WHO
DID
YOU
SEE
TODAY?

WHO DID YOU SEE TODAY?

THE POWER OF OUTRAGEOUS KINDNESS

DUSTIN SCHADT

B&H
PUBLISHING
BRENTWOOD, TENNESSEE

978-1-4300-8552-2

Published by B&H Publishing Group
Brentwood, Tennessee

Dewey Decimal Classification: 259
Subject Heading: CHRISTIAN LIFE \ MINISTRY \
INTERPERSONAL RELATIONS

Cover design by Matt Lehman. Image by Angelatriks/Shutterstock.
Author photo by Katie Colucci.

1 2 3 4 5 6 • 27 26 25 24

To:
Jimmy and Kristin
Kevin and Lynette
Nat and Tracy Millican
Mike and Debbie Schadt
And so many others.
Thank you for seeing me.

CONTENTS

FOREWORD

When I met Dustin Schadt, he was a college student at the University of Louisville. He was a baby Christian—a new believer who was eager to be discipled. He was energetic, interested, earnest, and intelligent. I was doing student ministry at a local church and had just started an evangelistic Bible study for fraternity and sorority students on Louisville's campus. Dustin was one of the first guys to show up.

Over the next several years Dustin and I built a deep and meaningful friendship. We met one on one for discipleship. We memorized Scripture together. We shared Christ with hundreds and hundreds of students in U of L's Greek system. We went on mission trips. I had the privilege of sharing the gospel with his girlfriend, April. She became a believer too.

Dustin and April spent time in our home, and my wife Kristin and I loved them both. They held our children, ate our food, and listened to our stories. I officiated their wedding, baptized April, helped them understand their call to ministry, and hired Dustin onto our church staff. I have taken tremendous joy in watching Dustin and April thrive in their marriage, work out their ministry calling, build their family, and grow their church. We have been friends for nearly twenty-five years. That's a lot of years, a lot of laughter, a lot of tears, a lot of love, and a lot of conversations.

Dustin has always been good at "seeing" people. I noticed this quality when he was a young adult. Other guys his age considered him a good and faithful friend. When Dustin would invite them to an event, guys would come because they knew Dustin cared about them. Dustin has gotten older but his sense of connection to people hasn't changed. When you are with Dustin, he always makes you feel like you are really important to him. He doesn't hurry. He asks good questions. He is thoughtful in his follow-ups. All these qualities make him a good husband, a good father, and a good pastor. No wonder his church is thriving: Who doesn't want a pastor like that? No wonder Dustin has a lot of deep friendships. Who doesn't want a friend who "sees" them? All that makes him the perfect person to write a book like this.

I hope you will be challenged by this book, as I am. The people in your life need to be "seen." And you should make the effort to "see" them. This kind of intentionality comes naturally to some people, but most of us have to work at it. My wife needs me to see her, my kids need me to see them, the people in my church need to be seen by me, and that doesn't count the people that God is going to put in my path. Plus, I need people to see me too.

Writing a book is really hard, it is. It is like putting pieces of your heart on paper. When you read this book, you will be reading more than Dustin's ideas—you will be reading Dustin's heart. You will be encouraged to see people the way that Jesus sees people. And hopefully, you will feel the eyes of God seeing you.

—Jimmy

Jimmy Scroggins and his wife Kristin have been married for twenty-nine years and have eight kids and four grand-kids. He is the lead pastor of Family Church—a multicultural, multigenerational, multisite church that meets in sixteen locations across three counties and four languages in South Florida. Jimmy has a MDiv and PhD from Southern Seminary in Louisville, Kentucky. Jimmy is the author of multiple books, including *Full Circle Parenting*, which he and Kristin wrote together.

1

SEE PEOPLE

On a beautiful (and hot) day in the neighborhood, Mr. Rogers took a moment to remove his shoes and soak his feet in a small pool of water. Rogers then invited Francois Clemmons, the friendly neighborhood policeman, to soak his feet alongside him. Clemmons was the first African American to hold a recurring role on a national children's program. They rested their feet together in the water and chatted about life. Mr. Rogers seemed to have a way of showing others their value. He drew in, focused, and responded to the individual people around him. Later, Clemmons said, "Fred Rogers not only was showing my brown skin in the tub with his white skin, but as I was getting out of that tub, he was helping me dry my feet."[1]

"He was helping me dry my feet."

"I think he was making a very strong statement," Clemmons said. "And I discovered a friend for life." Journalist Tom Junod said in a reflection on Rogers, "He practiced [kindness] like he practiced a musical instrument. I think he did the scales every day."[2]

• • •

Seeing people happens in countless everyday ways. Take, for instance, the time Sara's life intersected with her local postal service worker. Sara is bright, fun, kind, and a terrific mother. When I asked Sara if I could share her story, she said, "I don't have a spectacular story to tell—we've just become friends as she's grown to know me and my story and she knows I am a single mom like herself and has looked out for my son and me." One of the most beautiful things about Sara's story is that she thinks it's just ordinary. To Sara, it seems like something that you just do.

Do you know the name of the person who brings your mail? Sara sure does. Day after day, workers of the United States Postal Service visit nearly every person in the United States. In "rain, sleet, and snow" these tireless workers toil to bring birthday cards, junk mail, gifts, bills, and everything in between. They play a vital role in our communities, and each one of them has a story. To Sara, her postal worker isn't just "the mail lady." She is Marilyn. Over the course of thirteen years, Sara developed a dear friendship with Marilyn. On hot and humid Atlanta days, Marilyn could always count on Sara for a water, popsicle, or even lunch. Not only did Sara care for the person who brought the mail, but the mail lady also often ministered to Sara.

Upon Marilyn's retirement, Sara's whole neighborhood threw a party for their friend to honor this woman who had served them for many years. Kids painted signs celebrating Marilyn, this wonderful person they all came to know and love. I wonder how many days Marilyn drove through the neighborhood. How many pieces of mail did she deliver? How many rainy, hot, and even snowy days did she endure, hitting the brakes at each mailbox before accelerating to the next? It could be easy for a person and a neighborhood to forget, but this time, kindness and intentionality won the day.

Proverbs 11:25 (NIV) says, "A generous person will prosper; whoever refreshes others will be refreshed." Studies indicate that symptoms of struggling mental health are rising across individuals from every season of life, and especially among young people in our country. People feel unseen, depleted, and broken. The Lord is calling you and me to the people around us each day, to something so countercultural, unique, and powerful, that it just may make a dent in the sadness—He's called us to see people.

The Power of Washing Feet

What does the most powerful man in the room do when he understands that he is the most powerful man in the room? For Jesus, it meant showing care and practicing humility. Jesus didn't ask for service as the Son of God—instead, He served others. Jesus said in Matthew 20:28 "The Son of Man came not to be served but to serve, and to give his life as a ransom for many." Jesus gave us a visual example of this service when He gathered at a large religious festival with His followers. The Scriptures tell us that Jesus loved His followers "to the end" (John 13:1). When we think about the love of Jesus for His followers, we might sometimes think His love lacked the affection that we often feel in our love. This simply isn't true. Through the life of Jesus, He draws near in affection for His friends. He weeps at the death of a friend. He holds the hand of a little girl. He addresses a woman with a lifelong, debilitating, and embarrassing disease as a daughter.

Jesus knew His mission. He would endure temptation, give up Himself in death on a cross, and then rise victoriously from the grave. After a meal with His closest friends and followers, Jesus stood up, grabbed a towel, and tied it around His waist. Taking each of His friends' feet into His own hands, He washed their feet. I can't help but imagine the bewilderment of the group watching their leader stoop down to such a task, the task of a servant.

One of His closest followers rejected this offer, to which Jesus replied, "If I don't wash you, you have no part with me" (John 13:8 CSB). If we zoom out a bit on the story, we also see in attendance Judas Iscariot, who for a handful of coins would betray Jesus and hand Him over to be killed. And Jesus washed his feet too. In a world where vengeance and violence often ruled the day, Jesus told and showed us how to "love your enemies" (Matt. 5:44).

We see people first not because we decide that they deserve to be seen. We see people because every single person in the entire world matters to our heavenly Father. We often say within the church family something like, "As the Lord has been to us, so we will be to others." Maybe you've felt that kind of love. Maybe you've had someone draw their warm and inviting attention toward you. It seems when people spent time with Jesus, they felt like the only person in the room.

As children, we often had an adult place their focus on us. Maybe they sat on the floor with us, played a game, shared a meal, taught a math lesson, or showed us a skill. I'm sure you remember those childhood moments because they were meaningful to you. We never forget how good it feels to be seen and valued. Unfortunately, as adults we often go unseen and catch ourselves reflecting back to those long-ago moments when someone did see us.

But what if we could change that?

Tired from a long journey, Jesus sat down beside a well in the town of Samaria. As a Jewish man, Jesus would have had a history of strife to draw upon in relation to the Samaritan people. Jews and Samaritans held great animosity toward one another. As a woman from Samaria came to draw water, Jesus said to her, "Give me a drink." It's wild enough that a Jewish man would talk to a Samaritan, but further craziness that an upstanding religious man would engage in conversation with a woman known to make less than upstanding choices. Even Jesus's friends were dismayed. But Jesus persisted. He showed the woman He indeed is living water, not just quenching the palate in a moment, but the one who hydrates the soul forever. Jesus knew the woman, her sin, and her shortcomings—yet He saw her. He slowed down. He drew in.

Jesus stooped down to us, just like He met the Samaritan woman right where she was. He walked the earth as 100 percent man and 100 percent God, *at the same time.* The Son of

God, who created the stars in the sky and the waters of the sea, grew thirsty. He was tired, abandoned, beaten, and crucified. If Jesus could humble Himself to come all the way to earth from heaven and humble Himself to see us right where we are, surely we are meant to follow this example. Yet the question remains: *How* can we humble ourselves to see the people around us?

We live in a beautiful but fallen world. People are hurting and move around us each day feeling unseen and unloved. From 2009 to 2021, the share of American high-school students who say they feel "persistent feelings of sadness or hopelessness" rose from 26 percent to 44 percent, according to a new CDC study. This is the highest level of teenage sadness ever recorded.[3]

We pass dozens, hundreds, or even thousands of people every day—at crosswalks, subways, elementary schools, in neighborhoods, office parks, coffee shops, and gyms. Each has their own story with victories and struggles. Some of those people feel isolated, unseen and unknown. What are the names of a few of the people we pass each week? What might be on their minds and hearts?

Maybe you're great at seeing others, but you have a hard time *being* seen. Do you want others to see you? Do you truly want to be known? As scary as it may seem to let another person into our lives, we all want the authenticity and freedom that comes with knowing another person knows us—and accepts us. But perhaps you're a person who doesn't like attention, or maybe you're more introverted. I'd venture to guess you still want to be acknowledged, valued, and cherished. We all need the care of others.

Have you always wanted to truly mean something to another person? It may sound self-centered to say, "I want to mean something to someone." Understandable. But are we meant, then, to do the opposite? Are we to say, "I don't want to mean anything to anyone." Of course not. We are meant to mean something. As people made in the image of God, we have value, and it's good for us to recognize that in ourselves and in those around us. I hope you've had a person slow down and see you. If not, knowing the pain of going unseen may have taught you firsthand the power of seeing others—and you can do something about it.

Certainly, we shouldn't pursue a role of messiah to others. But we can point people to the true Messiah by living like He did. If we know what it means to be truly seen, we'll understand the power our care can have in another person's life. It's our privilege and our joy to serve others. You don't have to be Mr. Rogers to see others. You don't need a mailman, toy train, and an extra red sweater. You also don't have to be just like your hero. It's up to each of us (and all of us) to do what we can with what we have where we are—*every day.*

The greatest motivation we have for seeing others is the mind-boggling act of the Creator of the universe seeing us. The one who created the stars, sun, moon, and planets knew us before we were born and saw fit for His glory and our joy to meet us right where we are. In our brokenness and shame, our God stooped to our level in the person and work of His Son

Jesus. Through the broken body and shed blood of Jesus, our righteousness was purchased. But our hope didn't die with Christ on the cross. Our hope rose with Christ from the dead, so that in Him we also may rise. This is the good news of the gospel. Jesus said in John 15:12, "This is my commandment, that you love one another as I have loved you."

Sawubona

Sawubona (pronounced sŏw-uh-bone-uh) is a Zulu greeting that literally means, "We see you." Seeing a person, to a Zulu, is more than just physical eyesight. *Sawubona* means to acknowledge a person's humanity. The phrase uses the word "we" to acknowledge that when I see you, I am also representing all of my background including my experiences and my family. When I see you, I also recognize your experiences and family. "I see you" is more than a simple greeting. "I see you" means "I see the whole of you—your background, your passions, your pain, your strengths and weaknesses, and your future. You are valuable to me."[4] To see someone is to acknowledge their existence.

The proper response to Sawubona is "yebo (yeh-boh), sawubona," which means, "I see you, seeing me." How much insecurity exists today because people do not believe that someone sees them. As followers of Jesus, we don't live for the approval of others. However, God made us to know and be known. It is not good to be isolated. We are made to see and be seen.[5]

From Looking to Seeing

Is seeing others nothing more than saying hello, giving a nod, or exchanging pleasantries? I'm not sure how many lives have been transformed by saying howdy (do people still say howdy?) or talking about the weather. No, seeing others requires more.

On one occasion Jesus walked through the crowds, and a woman touched the fringe of His garment. Jesus asked His friends who touched Him, and they responded with surprise: "Jesus, there are many people here bumping and moving through the crowd. How in the world could You have felt just one person?" (Mark 5:31, author's paraphrase). Their reaction points to a mistake the disciples often made. They thought Jesus was just like them. The disciples moved through the crowd and felt many brushes against their shoulders and heard the hum of many voices. But Jesus didn't just see a crowd. He saw individual people. Unlike Jesus's friends, the woman knew that Jesus was different. She drew near to Jesus in fear and faith—a powerful combination.

Scripture doesn't say exactly why this woman was fearful. Maybe it was because in touching Jesus she caused Him, a Jewish teacher, to become ceremonially unclean. Or maybe she felt fear because the rush of the healing power of God in her life simply overwhelmed her. Or perhaps she feared rebuke for touching Jesus. In any case, she came trembling to Jesus and fell at His feet. How did Jesus respond? By calling her "daughter." He commended her faith and told her to go in peace. He saw this woman, right where she was.

How can we see others? After studying Jesus's interactions in the Gospels and learning from men and women in my own life who have loved others well, I like to define seeing people as a three-step process:

1. value
2. focus
3. respond

VALUE: Treasuring the Right Things

Jesus said, "Where your treasure is, there your heart will be also" (Matt. 6:21). What we value most becomes a compass guiding our direction. If we value money, we'll be drawn to work and compensation, and to the things or security money can bring. If we value our health, we'll be drawn to fitness and nutrition. If we value our image, we'll be drawn to what we wear and the company we keep. There may be nothing inherently wrong in money, fitness, or fashion, but we must be honest about what we truly value. What kind of value do we place on the people God has around us each day? Do we treasure others like they're made in the image of a loving God?

Have you ever had someone show you that you are valuable? My dad is a hard worker. I remember him coming home from work each day exhausted. Now that I'm a father of three teenagers and another elementary-age child, I understand why my parents were tired all the time. Physically tired, emotionally spent, and even grimy from the day, my dad would pull in the driveway in his old brown Honda Accord. I often would bombard him with two baseball gloves in hand, ready for him to crouch down as a catcher so I could practice my fastball. Almost every time, he would say yes. I'm right-handed, and my dad is left-handed, but he didn't have a glove of his own. He would take one of my baseball gloves and finagle it on his right hand. No matter how tiring the day had been, he was ready for an aspiring ten-year-old Nolan Ryan to fire baseballs at him. He valued me, and because of that, I remember those days like they were yesterday. My dad made me feel seen.

There are dozens, maybe even hundreds or thousands of people we pass each day who need to know they're valuable to their Creator. Showing value does not come from mere flattery or empty words. Showing value is not just empty fluff language. Rather, value is inherent in each one of us in who we are as image-bearers of God. We aren't valuable because of our image, vocation, abilities, or usefulness. We're valuable because we are created by God and for God.

Some people are more difficult to see than others. We wouldn't call them enemies (or maybe we would). They don't have a villain laugh and an evil lair. But they're tough. I pray that our God of grace would continue to open our hearts and minds and hands and feet to do what only the Spirit of God and the gospel of Jesus can do—move us to love our enemies. We'll talk more later in this book about some next steps in seeing those who are more difficult to see.

Seeing people doesn't mean that we over-empathize with people. Empathy is great. Overempathy is not. How do we know when we are over empathizing? We over-empathize when we compromise truth. I don't need to flatter a person to empathize. We must *not* affirm a person's unwise or unbiblical choices. Truth is kindness. What is important is that we are shrewd as a serpent and innocent as a dove in how we navigate tough decisions of delivering a word of rebuke or correction. Sometimes, seeing people means sharing a difficult truth.

FOCUS: Where Are You Looking?

An article on cell-phone distraction refers to "a dual-task activity that over 100 million drivers in the United States currently engage in: the concurrent use of a cell phone while operating a motor vehicle."[6] We are distracted people. We often point the finger at technology, but our phones are just a symptom of why our attention goes a hundred different ways. We have fears, desires, dreams, and worries that captivate our thoughts, and we want our mind elsewhere. It's no wonder we pass each other every day with little or no interaction. We have places to go, people to see, things to do, and sites to scroll. But what if the people we pass each day are the neighbors Jesus is calling us to? What if on our way, our "way" is the best place we can spend our time?

We pass by the grocery store clerk, fellow department employees, baristas, the guy across the street, the lady with the dog who walks by, and the guy who has a kiddo on the same sports team. We glance, wave, (maybe) remember their name, and then go on. How would things change if we took time to slow down, draw in, and give one of our most important assets of all—our attention? Value requires focus, so where are we looking?

While I was completing my masters degree, my wife and I had dear friends who often had us over for dinner. Did you have a season of life when you had to scrape and scrounge to make ends meet? We sure did. And this couple would host us in their home and make appetizers, salads, steaks, and dessert. What was even greater than the food (and boy, was it good) was the fact that this couple would slow down their lives as a busy mom and profitable business owner to spend time with us. They'd leave the mess in the kitchen, stand with no distraction, and just talk. No phones, no bragging, no checking their watches. It was as though we were the only people in the world. They listened, we laughed, and I'll never forget it. They were the right people at the right time to bring encouragement and significance into our lives.

I have a friend named Ross. He is from Scotland. Just imagine his amazing accent for a moment. He's a former college golfer who was led to Jesus by one of our faithful church members. Now Ross is a successful salesman with the gift of encouragement. One day I received a voicemail from him saying, "Dustin, brother. I was just driving by the church building and I thought of you. I prayed for you. I reflected on the sermons you deliver to us. And I'm thankful. I just wanted to call you and encourage you. I want to fill your heart with courage for the work of the Lord." I never thought of it that way—to encourage is to fill someone's heart with courage. That's exactly what Ross did for me on that day.

Here's the neat thing. You don't need to be wealthy to see others. Seeing people doesn't require education, money, status, or possessions. As human beings, we have the capacity to see others right where they are. We love stars of sports and entertainment—they may even be heroes to us. Chances are, though, celebrities haven't been the most influential people in our lives. That award goes to parents, coaches, pastors, and friends who choose to slow down and give us their attention. They fill our hearts with courage.

RESPOND: Moving from Observing to Serving

We want to value others, and we know it takes focus to do so. But how can we turn desire and knowledge into action? Our youngest son is a ball of energy and enthusiasm, and his fascination right now is Legos. I'm convinced 20 percent of my net worth is tied up in those tiny little bricks. If our little guy has been in a room, you know it; there'll be a field of little sharp bricks sticking out just waiting for someone's bare feet.

If we have been in a room, will someone know it? We don't have to be a lightning rod of energy, but are we outwardly postured enough that we leave a kind and gentle mark on every room we enter? Will there be a trail not of spiky Legos, but careful focus and attention drawn to the right person at the right time? Will someone know another person took the time to show the love and care of Jesus?

This may all sound a bit too easy—or it may seem a bit too difficult. You might be thinking, *How will I make time for others when I can hardly keep up with the demands of my own busy life?* We'll get into more of *how* to do this in the course of this book. For now, though, if you feel overwhelmed, start small. Look for the same grocery store clerk each time you visit. Stand in their line (even if it's longer). Ask them their name. I know, they have a name tag, but that doesn't make much of a connection. Maybe a compliment comes to your mind. Or maybe you ask briefly about family. Or you ask about their favorite snack food. Voilà—you have something to respond to.

"Okay," you might say, "Then what?" I buy them their favorite snack and their life changes? Maybe not. But over time, maybe you'll get the opportunity to tell them about Jesus and the difference He has made in your life. Maybe that day they felt lonely, overlooked, and discouraged and you brought a sense of love and kindness to their life. I think that's pretty awesome. Go ahead and multiply that moment from the superstore employee to your coworker, kids, spouse, roommate, or mechanic. We need to remember names, visit again, appropriately touch, buy small gifts, and hand-write notes.

David Livingstone was a Scottish physician and missionary to peoples all around Africa. Livingstone truly lived a life valuing and serving others. He sought to spread the gospel of Jesus and end slave trade. Despite persistent and debilitating sickness, Livingstone was determined not to leave Africa until his mission was complete. He eventually died in Africa from malaria and internal bleeding due to dysentery. Shortly after his death, two of his friends determined that his body belonged to Britain, but his heart belonged to Africa. The Chitambo people with whom he worked gave his body to be moved back to his homeland but buried his heart near a baobab tree in their area.

Livingstone said, "Sympathy is no substitute for action." Although we may be stirred emotionally when we see a need, it's what we do that ultimately makes a difference. So what *are* you and I going to do to really make a difference? We don't have to change the world in a moment, but we can respond to the people around us with love, compassion, and care.

• Reflection Questions •

1. Who would you point to in your life and say, "That person saw me"? How did they make you feel? What did they do? What did they say? Did they seem distracted, or did they focus on you?

2. Why don't people take time to slow down and see people?

3. What is the difference between showing a person their value as an image-bearer and mere flattery?

4. Why is it sometimes difficult to value others?

5. What stories of Jesus seeing people can you recall?

6. Who can you call, text, or write—today—and fill their heart with courage?

2

JESUS SAW PEOPLE

*"Aslan is a lion—the Lion, the great Lion." "Ooh,"
said Susan. "I'd thought he was a man. Is he—
quite safe? I shall feel rather nervous about
meeting a lion." . . . "Safe?" said Mr. Beaver . . .
"Who said anything about safe? 'Course he isn't
safe. But he's good. He's the King, I tell you."*[1]
—C. S. Lewis, *The Lion, the Witch and the Wardrobe*

Chris works with his hands, wears T-shirts every day, and asks great questions about Jesus. His accent gives away his Long Island upbringing, and I enjoy hearing him talk about the differences between the city and our suburban life. We often talk about his successful business endeavors, church peculiarities, woodworking, travel, and why things are the way they are. Chris has become a dear friend to me. We've built things together and had dinner in each other's homes. One of my favorite things about Chris is that he's a regular guy. There's no pretense or judgment with Chris. He has a great laugh and a humble presence that is warm and inviting. I've never had the sense Chris feels he has everything figured out. He is always learning, thinking, and growing.

Chris's wife, Maria, is just as wonderful. Raised in a multicultural family, she has a beautiful range of life experience. With a bright smile and long, dark, curly hair, Maria's kind demeanor provides a welcoming presence to everyone she encounters. As an occupational therapist, Maria works one-on-one with people to restore their work and daily routines. She spends her days helping people of all ages and backgrounds redevelop their fine motor skills. I can imagine Maria sitting close to one of her patients, placing a pen into a hand, and then guiding the hand to learn to write again. Chris says of Maria, "She spends her days holding people's hands."

We see this same picture often in Scripture. When Jesus healed Peter's mother-in-law, He healed as He held onto her hand. Just imagine, the Son of God, Creator of all things, reaching out His strong, perhaps calloused hand. What did Jesus's hands feel like? Rough like a carpenter? Strong like a father? Jesus extended the hand that would later receive nails for our sake. In this moment, with her hand in His, He healed a woman's broken body. Not long after this encounter, Jesus healed a little girl. What did Jesus do as He healed her? He held her hand. The Son of God knelt next to a child's bed, simply holding her hand. There's just something special about a person who holds your hand, sees you, and serves you.

Unsurprisingly, Chris and Maria are always looking for ways to see and serve others. A few years ago, they caught a vision for the care of foster children in our community. Chris was ready to foster before Maria. Maria wasn't able to have biological children, and she told me that she's felt the pain and loss of missing out on motherhood in more ways than she can count. But over time, the Lord moved Maria's heart just as He had moved Chris's, and they took steps to meet this need in our community. They attended a foster care information meeting, did home studies, and engaged in the many training meetings required to welcome precious children into a loving home.

By God's grace, our church welcomes several kids on Sunday morning who are currently in the care of foster parents. Faith is a single woman in our church who follows Jesus and works as a writer for a nonprofit organization. She too felt a call to foster and began the process of training and certification. We saw her walk into church one Sunday alone, and then the following Sunday, there she was with a little guy skipping alongside her.

Accepting foster children into your home happens without much notice—sometimes only hours or days. So, Chris and Maria simply appeared one Sunday with a beautiful little girl in their arms. Chris and Maria are regular people, working regular jobs and leading a fairly normal life. But the call to see people the way Jesus sees us led them to open their home in an extraordinary way. When they walked through the doors with their foster daughter, their whole faces radiated with joy. Even though we had shared meals together, laughed, cried, and prayed alongside Chris and Maria, we had never witnessed such a glow on their faces as when they met "Cheeks"—the nickname Chris and Maria gave to this sweet little girl. Cheeks, like most kids in foster care, had biological parents who'd experienced difficult and dark days. I personally watched Cheeks go from a tremendously shy, fearful, and suspicious little girl into a skipping, dancing, singing little bundle of excitement and curiosity.

For Cheeks, days in care turned into weeks, and weeks turned into months. One of the realities of foster care is that foster parents have zero control over the circumstances of children we welcome into our homes. Children are often caught up between courts, laws, and unfortunate family situations. As much as they loved Cheeks living in their home, Chris and Maria never knew how long it would last. I do something simple with every family in our church who begins the foster journey. I have them raise a hand, and repeat after me, "These children do not belong to me. They belong to the Lord. I do not have control over them, or their circumstances, or their biological parents. Lord, I trust You."

During their time with Cheeks, Chris and Maria also cared for her biological mother. They drove her to appointments, rehabilitation clinics, and job interviews. They brought meals, encouraged her in times of despair, and even helped buy her a vehicle. Most would say that Chris and Maria had gone above and beyond in their sacrifice and care for others. Opening yourself to the possibility—or certainty—of pain and stepping into the unknown are everyday practices of foster parents.

As if their investment into this family wasn't enough, Chris and Maria went one giant step further.

They wanted to make sure Cheeks was set up for care for as long as they could provide. After consulting with a local attorney, Chris and Maria legally adopted Cheeks's mother as their own child—a twenty-something-year-old, facing her own set of struggles. Only God could dream up a plan to make Chris and Maria parents by the unconventional means of adopting an adult child. They had a child to call their own and a grandchild to whom they could show the love and care of Jesus for years to come.

Today, Cheeks is back in the care of her biological family. One of the first objections to fostering children is thinking, *I don't know if I could give them up once they were in my care.* This is, of course, understandable. But after looking back, Chris and Maria told me they have no regrets. They even wonder if they could have done more. There are days they weep, and days they laugh with joy over the memories they shared. But Chris and Maria lived selflessly and generously with their time, their home, and their entire lives because they grasped this incredible truth: seeing people changes the lives of others, but it changes us too.

Normal People, Extraordinary God

This isn't a book about superheroes. This isn't a book about foster care, although foster care is a great way to see people and step into their lives in a meaningful way. This isn't a book about talent, or aptitude, or even about having a "big heart." It's more than that. This is a book about what we're made for, even if we consider ourselves "just regular people." Chris and Maria are both extraordinary and tremendously ordinary at the same time, and look what God did with their "regular" lives. He answered their prayers in an unconventional way and richly blessed another family through their obedience.

We didn't have to clean up our lives first for Jesus to accept us, and we don't have to have it all together in order to follow His example. The crew Jesus assembled to be His first disciples didn't have the best spiritual résumés. He gathered a tax collector, gritty fishermen, and even one who would later betray Him, and they almost never understood what He was teaching about Himself. Yes, after Jesus's ascension, God used them mightily. Jesus often uses ordinary people to do extraordinary things.

Jesus can use us *right now*.

In Isaiah 42:6 God says, "I am the LORD; I have called you in righteousness; I will take you by the hand and keep you; I will give you as a covenant for the people, a light for the nations." We've been called to this. Our God takes us by the hand. He sees us. He knows us. He loves us. In our moment of deepest despair, He meets us individually and with kindness.

The Lord doesn't ask us to take off our shoes and clean ourselves up before we come into His house. He runs to us from afar with arms wide open. Then He gives us a job. He asks us to do for others what He has done for us.

We are His *covenant* people. A covenant can be thought of as a *super* promise. God super-promises that we are His, and He is our God. And then He sends us out as a "light for the nations" (Isa. 49:6). The nations need the light of Jesus shining through us unclouded by our own ambition and agenda. It's dark out there, but the Light is coming.

Today, there are tens of thousands of "Cheeks" in our country and around the world. There are mail ladies, coworkers, sisters, coaches, players, teachers, fellow students, and family members who believe, right now, that no one sees them. There is only one thing worse than feeling lost: feeling that no one is looking for you while you're lost. In the kingdom of Christ, we are sent to be finders. We are the ones who look for others when they feel lost and help bring them into a home, a family, and a beautiful future.

Jesus Sees Us

What would it have been like to watch Jesus move through a crowd? When I read the Bible, I see that Jesus had a destination in mind, but He didn't mind being interrupted on the journey. Small "distractions" along the way displayed purpose in themselves. Before jumping to the specifics of *how* we can see people, let's answer *why* we should see people. The "why" comes to us from the example of Jesus.

When I think about characters in the Bible I can relate to, the disciple Peter comes to mind. Some biblical characters, like Mary, seem to radiate gentleness, patience, and godliness. When Mary learned she would be the one to carry Jesus to His birth, she sang a beautiful song: "My soul magnifies the Lord, and my spirit rejoices in God my Savior, because he has looked with favor on the humble condition of his servant. Surely, from now on all generations will call me blessed" (Luke 1:46–48 CSB).

Peter, on the other hand, seemed to have a foot-shaped mouth. He didn't speak with elegance, and he was prone to say the wrong thing at the wrong time. Jesus often reminded His disciples that His mission would end with suffering and death. Peter rebuked Jesus for this type of speech. Imagine the creation (Peter) rebuking the Creator (Jesus). What a mess.

I played middle school basketball. And when I say "play," I mean I was on the team. I had a jersey, Jordans, and a nice warm spot at the very end of the bench. I sat so long so I often had cramps in my calves simply from sitting so long. In fifth grade, I did bank in a 3-pointer, and that was the only time I scored (or shot the ball) all season. LeBron James often plays against the team in our city, the Atlanta Hawks. It would be ludicrous if I showed up early to the next game in order to give LeBron tips on his jump shot. Similarly, Peter, in his spiritual deficiency, had no authority to coach Jesus. Even so, Jesus was patient and kind in His interactions with Peter.

On another occasion, Peter saw Jesus walking on water. In response, Peter jumped out of a boat in order to walk after Jesus. Because of his lack of faith, Peter sank into the water. Peter told Jesus he wouldn't allow his feet to be washed by Jesus. Jesus rebuked him. Peter also tried to build temples not only to Jesus, but also to Moses and Elijah, essentially equating the importance of the three. A satire website once published a humorous article with the title, "Apostle Peter Cringes While Reading Gospel Accounts of All the Dumb Stuff He Did."[2]

And still, Jesus was long-suffering with Peter. To be fair, Jesus did once call Peter Satan. If you're wondering if you've said the right thing to Jesus, and then Jesus calls you Satan, what you said was not the right thing. Despite this teachable moment with Peter, Jesus displayed an enormous amount of grace toward Peter's posture of humility and repentance. He didn't humiliate Peter at every opportunity—and there were many opportunities. Rather, Jesus knew the long plan He had for Peter's life.

Peter often fell short. He said things he regretted. But Jesus didn't give up on Peter. Jesus eventually gave Peter a nickname—rock. This nickname wasn't intended in jest—like calling a big muscular guy "Tiny." Jesus knew the power of God at work in Peter's life, and He wanted to give him a name fitting for his massive place in the kingdom. The name "Peter" and the word "rock," in Greek, sound similar. Jesus said, "And I tell you, you are Peter [*Petros*, in Greek], and on this rock [*petra*, in Greek] I will build my church, and the gates of hell shall not prevail against it. I will give you the keys of the kingdom of heaven, and whatever you bind on earth shall be bound in heaven, and whatever you loose on earth shall be loosed in heaven" (Matt. 16:18–19).

Through all of Peter's struggles and shortcomings, Jesus saw Peter.

One of the many things I love about Jesus is that He didn't treat people the way they treated Him. Jesus didn't dispense grace based on who He deemed to deserve it. And that's a really good thing, because none of us deserve the grace of Jesus. If we deserved grace, then it wouldn't be grace at all.

Jesus's heart is full of grace toward those who follow Him. He sees the long plan for our lives, just as He saw Peter's.

We have an 80-pound goldendoodle. When a family moves to the north Atlanta suburbs, they give to you, as standard issue, a Honda Odyssey van and a jumping, leaping goldendoodle. We love Windsor, but we don't often love taking her for walks. Part of the dog-walking duty (no pun intended) involves cleaning up after her. It's a crazy picture every dog owner knows well—unrolling a little bag and picking up the mess.

I confess I often imagine Jesus forgiving my sin while He holds His nose and looks the other way, the way I must look when cleaning up after our dog. I picture a look of disgust after He, yet again, has to forgive my sin. I've even imagined forgiveness as the task Jesus procrastinates because it robs Him of emotional energy, like He keeps moving it to the bottom of His task list as something He'll get to tomorrow. But this is far from the truth. It is not how Jesus approaches forgiving us.

If Jesus (or we) offer grace based on merit, it's not grace we're offering. Grace is receiving what we do not deserve. "In him [Jesus] we have redemption through his blood, the forgiveness of our trespasses, according to the riches of his grace, which he lavished upon us in all wisdom and insight" (Eph. 1:7–8). Jesus richly pours out His grace on His people because of His character, not because of our merit. He isn't stingy with grace. He isn't rationing His grace because He never runs out of it.

In Hebrews 12:2 (CSB), the author tells us, "Jesus [is] the pioneer and perfecter of our faith. For the joy that lay before him, he endured the cross, despising the shame, and sat down at the right hand of the throne of God." What did Jesus do for joy? He endured the agonizing cross. Dispensing grace through His broken body and shed blood is the very thing He loves to do—not because He loves pain, but because He loves us enough to give the ultimate sacrifice. Dane Ortlund, in his book *Gentle and Lowly*, explains it this way: "'For the joy.' What joy? What was waiting for Jesus on the other side of the cross? The joy of seeing his people forgiven."[3]

Thomas Goodwin phrases it like this: "Christ's own joy, comfort, happiness, and glory are increased and enlarged by his showing grace and mercy, in pardoning, relieving, and comforting his members here on earth."[4] If we want to see the joy of Christ increased, we must run to Him for forgiveness and grace. Offering forgiveness is the very thing He loves to do, the thing He was willing to die for. In John 15:11 (CSB), Jesus tells His disciples to abide in Him "so that my joy may be in you and your joy may be complete." Jesus invites us to His work on the cross for us. When we draw near to the foot of the cross, we see more clearly the heart of Christ toward us, sinners.

There's a quick little statement in Matthew 10 that's easy to miss. Jesus rallies His twelve apostles, the men who will turn the world upside down, and fills them with instruction on how they're going to do it. He tells them to heal the sick, raise the dead, cleanse lepers, and cast out demons. Those are the tasks. Then He gives them a "why," and it's only seven words long. Again, it's easy to miss, but it provides booming motivation for those who want to change the world, even when it's difficult. Jesus tells them:

"You received without paying; give without pay." (Matt. 10:8)

We received without paying. God gives us grace based not on our ability to pay Him back. God gives us His own Son. We paid nothing. So what do we do? Give without pay. Receive Jesus. Give life.

Most simply, I see others best when I understand that I have been seen by Jesus—*even while I didn't deserve it*. In light of the grace I've been given, how can I withhold grace from those around me? Scott Sauls, in his book *A Gentle Answer*, says this of Jesus: "When Jesus recognized people who recognized their own spiritual bankruptcy, he did not shame or belittle them—though he had every right to do so. Instead, he had a way of making them feel like the most significant, esteemed, and beloved people in the world."[5]

One of our regular church attenders once reached out to me for a meeting. At this point in my ministry, I hadn't yet learned to avoid meetings without knowing the agenda. "Blind" meetings like that can (sometimes) turn into an ambush for a pastor. This particular meeting took place at a local coffee shop and, after a few moments of pleasantries, I was informed by this person that they rarely (if ever) get anything out of my preaching. I don't know if you know this about pastors, but we can be insecure about our preaching. It's a vulnerable task that is a primary responsibility in our role, and most pastors feel they could be a lot better at it.

I could have responded with grace, but I didn't. I felt my blood pressure rise, and indignation infiltrated my heart. I didn't explode on him, or respond with coarse words, but I did clam up and walk away with less than gracious thoughts. However, that exchange (and others like it), together with the Word of God and His Holy Spirit, show me that I have a long way to go in looking like Jesus. I distinctly remember the conviction on my heart over my anger at this person and this meeting. By God's grace I determined next time I'll answer, "You know what, I wonder if people are connecting while I'm preaching. How can I do a better job and better serve Jesus?" Jesus sees me in my rebellion and responds with grace, and I pray I can do the same.

We See Others

After a career in the NFL, Dr. Derwin Gray planted Transformation Church in Charlotte, North Carolina. Derwin is passionate about equipping pastors and their churches to pursue multiethnic unity. In a podcast interview with Carey Nieuwhof, Dr. Gray explained that Jesus was an "everybody type of a person."[6] Jesus didn't draw near only to those like Himself. He drew near to the rich, poor, outcast, religious, and unreligious. He wasn't afraid of people's hard questions, and He didn't shy away from those who others shied away from. Jesus truly was an everybody type of a person.

If I want to live like Jesus, I have to ask myself, "Am I an everybody type of a person?" I'm now in my forties. To some, that seems old. To others, I'm just getting started. There was a time in my life when I didn't choose all the people with whom I would interact. I had teammates on my baseball team, classmates in my university, and others who lived in apartments around me. For a season, I worked several jobs at one time, and most of my days were spent with my coworkers and supervisors.

But now, I have more freedom to select the people with whom I interact. I go to the places I like and choose the people I spend my free time with. While there's nothing wrong with having committed friendships with people who have common interests, I often feel I'm missing out on the breadth and diversity of people I knew in my younger years. It's as though I've subconsciously navigated toward people that are just like me.

If you zoom out to see the whole scope of the life of Jesus, it's difficult to pinpoint a specific type of person He drew near to. He didn't pick His friends based on convenience or demographics. Rather, Jesus drew near to the broken-hearted, weak, and needy.

The apostle Paul in Philippians 2:5 teaches us to "have this mind among yourselves, which is yours in Christ Jesus." This Greek word for "mind" is also translated as "attitude." We are to have the mind and attitude of Jesus. On sports teams, coaches often tell their players that attitude is everything. Their attitude determines both their preparation for the game and how well they execute the game itself. In life, our attitudes are also contagious, spreading to our "teammates," people we know and work with, and even into the "stands" of the strangers and acquaintances who observe our lives.

We want the same attitude as Jesus. Paul tells us about the attitude of Jesus in the verses before and after verse 5. Verse 4 says, "Everyone should look not to his own interests, but rather to the interests of others" (CSB). It's easy to focus on our own interests. We can quickly determine what will move us toward our goals and then focus on the path we'll need to take to arrive at those goals. But Jesus invites us to be interrupted. Living like Jesus means stepping off the path to our own goals because our interests are not the most important thing. We are called to look to the interests of others.

I believe the word *interests* in this verse is purposefully vague. The interests of others may be spiritual in nature. People need to hear about Jesus's gospel work. Interests may also be hobbies, family, recreation, or work. It is good and right to care about things other people care about.

Transformers were a vital part of my childhood, and Optimus Prime was a household staple. This was before the days of on-demand TV and Netflix. You had to know the time the show would air and sit patiently for the turn of the hour. I tuned in to the *Transformers* TV show every chance I got, and my action figures often made their way into the bathtub and the backyard. I distinctly remember my mother folding laundry while I gave her play-by-play recaps of the most recent *Transformer* episode. She would nod her head like she was fully invested in the mystery of how a jet fighter could transform into a crime-fighting robot. She listened to me, and I felt seen.

Somewhere along the way, we stop being mindful of the interests of others. It feels counterintuitive to get inquisitive about a topic in which we have no interest. In order to have an interest, something must *seem* interesting, right? There are certain topics that pique my interest—travel, my kids' sports, theology, and CrossFit are all topics I could talk about for hours. On the other hand, my wife likes to watch British television dramas. You know what I don't find interesting? British television dramas. But over time, I've learned to sit with her, quietly tune in, and engage with her favorite TV shows. This one truth has helped my selfish heart:

It matters to me because it matters to you.

I'm not asking us to constantly pretend to be interested in things that don't hold our attention. I do believe we should care enough about the people in our lives that we're willing to spend time in their world, simply because we love them. It's not about loving the particular topic—it's about loving the person behind it. It's not always about the what, but the who.

I wanted to think about a way to best communicate to our youngest son what it means to lay our interests aside for the sake of others. Sometimes it's difficult for him, just like it is for me, to put others ahead of himself. But I desperately want my four children to have the mind of Jesus. I asked my son to hold up his hands like he is holding on to his interests and I asked him to think of putting his interests in his hands. Then I told him to take his hands and move those interests to the side, and then point his fingers out forward toward a person who would be sitting in front of him. We put our own Legos, Wild Kratts, and dirt bikes aside for the sake of taking up the interests of others.

Paul further describes the attitude of Jesus in Philippians 2:6 (CSB): "Who [Jesus], existing in the form of God, did not consider equality with God as something to be exploited." Jesus was 100 percent God and 100 percent man. *Kenosis* is the theological term for what Jesus did in choosing not to deploy the full capacity of His divinity for His own gain. For example, Jesus didn't overpower the soldiers who came to arrest Him. He allowed Himself to be taken, for our sake and for the glory of His Father. Peter, in contrast, took out a sword and cut off the ear of one soldier. Later, Peter denied ever knowing Jesus. Peter was ready to kill for Jesus, but Peter wasn't ready to die for Jesus. In the ultimate act of kenosis, Jesus gave up His own life on the cross:

> And being found in human form, he humbled himself by becoming obedient to the point of death, even death on a cross. Therefore God has highly exalted him and bestowed on him the name that is above every name, so that at the name of Jesus every knee should bow, in heaven and on earth and under the earth, and every tongue confess that Jesus Christ is Lord, to the glory of God the Father. (Phil. 2:8–11)

Wealth, time, talent, and energy can be gifts from the Lord. Selfishness tells us to consider how we might leverage it all for our own pleasure and goals. The way of Jesus moves us to consider how we might instead leverage our good gifts from the Lord for the joy of others and the glory of Jesus.

If Jesus stands ready, with the welcoming of the broken-hearted as His great joy, then He may want us to extend that same warm welcome to others. What if the selflessness that brought Christ the greatest joy was intended for my joy as well? What if we take a different perspective on our most prized possessions—wealth, time, talent, and energy—and consider putting them in the hands of the Lord? As we've seen in the stories of ordinary people in this book, He can do more than we can imagine when we give Him access to our lives and resources. What if there is greater joy in leveraging our gifts for others than we could ever find in leveraging them for ourselves? Jesus can use us to reach a world around us—a world that needs to know that the love we have experienced through Jesus is available for them too.

The perfect Christ, the righteous Son of God, sees us. He doesn't just tolerate us. He loves us. He draws near. He longs for our hope, joy, and peace that comes from knowing and following Him. He truly is a friend of sinners and welcomes those who humbly draw close to Him. Jesus invites us into a relationship with Himself, and then propels us to invite others to experience His love. The apostle Paul reminded the church at Rome that they shouldn't look down on others who might be weaker in the faith. Instead, Paul told them to "welcome one another as Christ has welcomed you, for the glory of God" (Rom. 15:7).

See People like John Powell Saw People

The truck burst into flames after colliding into another vehicle. Quickly, onlookers collected on U.S. Highway 75. Two of those onlookers were thirty-eight-year-old John Powell, a father of four, and his friend. John often found himself in a situation where he was unable to simply stand by. He had to help. John saw people, right where they were. As John and his friend assisted the endangered driver, John was struck by another vehicle and was killed.

The driver in the burning truck survived.

John's church described his heroism as "an act in the image of His sacrificial Savior." Theologian Russell Moore said of Powell, "John was one of the best men I ever knew—sweet-tempered, humble, absolutely devoted to Jesus, his wife, and their kids. He was everything I would want any of my sons to be when they grow up." Author and pastor Dean Inserra said, "He never cared about being known. Faithfully plowed daily as a family man and local church pastor. He did not sweat what many sweat." Pastor Peyton Hill remembered John this way: "A minute with John would always help calibrate me to what actually matters."

One of John's favorite activities was tossing around a baseball. Each year, John and his friends attended a large annual meeting, and each year John and a couple friends made time away from conference commitments to play catch. Nearly a year after the accident, John's friends organized a larger baseball toss event in his honor. On a warm June morning, nearly a hundred people gathered to remember John for the loving husband, father, and friend that he was. I had the privilege of attending this event. As I threw back and forth with friends, I could hear the distinctive sound of baseballs hitting gloves echoing behind the laughs and joyful conversation on the field. John's wife, Katherine, threw out a ceremonial first pitch to John's dad, who in memory wore John's beloved baseball glove.

Thirteen days before the highway accident, John preached his final sermon. John urged the congregation, "How could we pray that God would have compassion on those that need it while not having compassion on them ourselves? It would be like praying for someone who got robbed and beaten and thrown into a ditch alive while we pass on our way to wherever we're going."[7]

Every one of us will deliver a final sermon. You may not be a preacher, but we are all sending a message with our lives. We only have a divinely determined number of days to live our message. Every day we pass by people with dreams, hurts, aspirations, pains, and a story. We can't see everyone. But all of us can see someone.

• Reflection Questions •

1. Jesus saw individuals in a powerful way. What story of Jesus seeing people resonates with you?

2. Jesus seemed to be interruptible. What prevents you from being interruptible?

3. How do you imagine Jesus's interaction when we come to Him with our sin?

4. Take a moment, sit quietly, and repeat the concept of Matthew 10:8: "We received without paying. Give without pay." Can you think of an example of a person who gave to you without expecting repayment? What impact did that make in your life?

5. What do you think it means to be an "everybody type of person"? What keeps you from living as an "everybody type of person"?

6. Write down the names of three people in your everyday life who you can work to see more like Jesus sees them.

3

VALUE

*Everyone will be forgotten, nothing we do
will make any difference, and all good
endeavors, even the best, will come to
naught. Unless there is God. If the God of
the Bible exists, and there is a True Reality
beneath and behind this one, and this life is
not the only life, then every good endeavor,
even the simplest ones, pursued in response
to God's calling, can matter forever.*[1]
—Tim Keller

What is your favorite possession? Mine is a well-worn, cardinal
red fitted hat from my alma mater, the University of Louisville.
To be honest, it's a bit tight on me now. Has my head gotten bigger? But that's okay, because what makes the hat valuable to
me isn't the fit, or even the magnificent Cardinal logo. My red
hat was the exact hat that I was wearing when I met my wife,
April, in 1999 at a fraternity rush event. With all the courage
that I could muster, I walked up to her (with that red hat on
backward) and said, "Hey." It was the best line I could come up
with at the moment. So that silly hat has value to me. I protect

it in a special place in my closet. I tell stories about it. Every now and then, I'll even cram it back on my head and say "Hey" to April. She isn't impressed.

I bet there's something you've held onto year after year, because we all take care of things we value. We prioritize our time and resources around what carries the most weight in our lives. We talk about what we value, whatever it is: our career, morals, vehicles, homes, family, money, or even sleep. What we value drives our desires, fears, worries, and energy. Value is powerful.

Every day, we pass by people—the guy pumping gas across from us, the couple walking by on our daily walk or run, classmates in our math class, the kids who ride their bikes down the street, and the parent in the carpool line in front of us. Each one of them wants to *feel* valued. Some people are at a high point in their story. Others are struggling. Alone with their thoughts, people may ask themselves, "Does anyone really care about me? What if people knew the real me? Would they run from me? Would they gasp? Does anyone struggle like this?" These are real questions I hear in my office and in coffee and lunch meetings every week.

I know people have these questions. I see it in people who visit my office and I see it in my own heart. I know I need people to see me. I hurt, I struggle, and I wonder if anyone feels the same. As much as I want to be independent, autonomous, and free, I know that I need others to value, support, and care about me. It's tough to reach out and say, "Can you please encourage me?" Our need to be seen goes deeper than sentimentality or affection. We are wired to crave real connections with real people. Our heavenly Father made us that way.

Imago Dei

Our God is a beautiful Creator. He made the Himalayan mountains, sunsets over Santa Monica, and the Victoria Falls on the Zambezi River. He crafted amazing animals of every size and shape. But what we see from the book of Genesis is that we, His people, are the greatest creation of all. We are, "very good indeed" (Gen. 1:31 CSB).

God created us in His image and according to His likeness. To put it more succinctly, we are created as "image-bearers" of our God. This means that we are a little bit like God, and we represent Him on earth. What a life-changing truth! Because God's value is infinite, we, as His creations, are valuable too. We are magnificent tiny reflections of a God who spoke the entire world into existence and created each of us. Every person is valuable—period. When we believe this, it changes the way we see every single person, including ourselves.

We aren't valuable simply because we are useful to society. We aren't valuable because we are beautiful, strong, smart, fast, wise, or wealthy. We are valuable because we bear the image of our God. And here is why that's so important—we aren't valuable based on our usefulness. Every person, regardless of ability (or disability), age, socioeconomic status, ethnicity, or talent is an image-bearer of God.

We are not just animals. Animals are enslaved to their desires. Have you ever tried to train a dog to stop chasing squirrels? Have you ever left food on your counter, only to discover that your precious pup is an uncontrollable counter surfer? The life of a creature is lived meal to meal and nap to nap. As awesome as German shepherds, goldendoodles, Labradors, and English setters may be, they are still animals, creatures who are driven merely by their senses. They are slaves to their eyes, bellies, and instincts.

People, on the other hand, have the ability to contemplate how we got here. We ask questions of right and wrong. We fight for justice. We build hospitals, refugee centers, and churches to help others and make Jesus known. We teach children mathematics, languages, and history. We marvel at sunsets and laughing babies. We have the capacity to know and pursue our Creator. Our knowledge of something greater than ourselves, a heavenly Father and Creator, tells us that life is more than just moving from pleasure to pleasure. We are not just instinctual. Romans 1 tells us that we have an innate sense of the existence and character of God. Romans 1:20 shows, "For his invisible attributes, namely, his eternal power and divine nature, have been clearly perceived, ever since the creation of the world, in the things that have been made. So they are without excuse." As beloved image-bearers of our heavenly Father, we aren't made just to consume, procreate, and disappear. We have an essence and a purpose. If we're honest, we all feel it deep down—we were created for something more, something that matters. If you attend a secular university, your classes might

dig into biology, sociology, and the writings of well-known phi-
losophers. If you attend a suburban high school, you'll see students form culturally agreed-upon norms about who we are.
But God, through His Word, paints a different picture of our
value and purpose. Genesis 1:26–27 says it this way: "Then God
said, 'Let us make man in our image, after our likeness.' . . . So
God created man in his own image, in the image of God he created him; male and female he created them."

We all love a good origin story—LeBron James, Frodo, Taylor
Swift, Luke Skywalker, Tim Tebow, and Katniss Everdeen all
came from somewhere. We all have an origin story that began
long before our birth. Jeremiah 1:5 tells us, "Before I formed you
in the womb I knew you, and before you were born I consecrated
you." God knew us, long before our process of cellular mitosis.
He knew our eye color, height, strengths, and talents. He knew
us, long before we or anyone else knew us. He created us. Our
heavenly Father is our Creator. And yet, mankind is the masterpiece. And furthermore, mankind is a beloved masterpiece.

We have a dear younger couple in our church who has
been in the international adoption process for quite a while.
They are currently waiting to meet face-to-face their precious
little girl who lives in South Africa. They have pictures and
written records of their daughter, but they've yet to meet her.
Their daughter recently turned four years old, and instead
of moping about without their little girl, this young couple
decided to throw a big birthday party for her. They dressed
up, had a beautiful cake made with her name and birthday,
and celebrated—before they ever even met her. Lord willing,

they'll be traveling soon loaded with anticipation and a marvelous story of celebration to share. Our heavenly Father loved us before we first expressed our love for Him. Before He formed us, He knew us and loved us. God demonstrates His own love for us, that while we were still sinners Christ died for us (Rom. 5:8).

Adam and Eve

The first people, Adam and Eve, lived in a beautiful world. Plants were lush and fruit-bearing. Trees soared toward the radiant sunshine. The ground swelled with water, and sparkling rivers flowed through the land. Adam and Eve lived together in harmony with creation, each other, and God. Genesis goes on to show us that God gave human beings two initial tasks.

First, He told them to fill the earth. This task shows us we are made to invest our lives into precious children. Multiplication and the care of the next generation are a form of worship. Psalm 127:3 tells us children are a beautiful gift from the Lord. When you serve as a super aunt or funcle (fun uncle), welcome a child into your home through fostering, care for biological children, nurture young ones as a grandparent, or serve with little ones in your church or school, you are doing exactly what God created you to do. We can diaper change to the glory of God. A round of the Chutes and Ladders board game can offer a kind of worship. Demonstrating our presence by listening to a fifteen-year-old is an act of love unto our Savior.

Second, the Lord tells Adam and Eve to go to work. In Genesis 1:28, the Lord puts forth a mandate:

> "... have dominion over the fish of the sea and over the birds of the heavens and over every living thing that moves on the earth."

Your résumé probably doesn't list "hunter and gatherer" as your last place of employment. While we may not fish or hunt as a profession (regrettably, for some), this call is in principle a call to work. Work is created to be good. We are told to "have dominion," or to take what is chaotic and bring it into order. We exercise dominion when we take what is in the world and fashion it into something useful and beautiful for mankind.

Even if you find yourself in a field outside of your main passion, you still have the opportunity to worship God with the attitude that you have toward your occupation. We can contribute to the flourishing of our society, care for coworkers, display Christlikeness in the midst of conflict and challenge, and live on mission.

We reflect the image of our Creator when we work well. Colossians 3:23 says, "Whatever you do, work heartily, as for the Lord and not for men." Our work gives us purpose, and our rest reminds us to reflect on and worship God. When we work well, we glorify Jesus. We get in trouble, though, when we take any one aspect of image-bearing and make it the ultimate thing.

Therefore, we derive our value not based on our income, occupation, or reputation. As we surrender to our heavenly Father, our move is not from a lack of value to a place of value. Rather, our surrender leads us to a life of purpose from our original place of value—the image of God.

You and everyone around you already has value. The value of others is not based on their ability to contribute to your own personal well-being. Understanding who we are as image-bearers leads us to believe that the man with the cardboard sign at the end of the off-ramp has the same value to the Father as the heavily guarded politician shuffled around on private jets.

We must not allow our own self-image to rob us of the understanding that we are fearfully and wonderfully made. Whether we are in shape or out of shape, our heavenly Father loves us just the same. We are His. John 3:16 shows us that God loves everyone in the world. He doesn't love us based on performance. He loves us because we are His possession. You have value that cannot be invalidated by your decisions or taken by another person. Your value is inherent—it is built in.

When we truly understand our value, we can live a life of purpose. We aren't just a collection of molecules. We were not made simply to draw breath and draw a paycheck. We are little mirrors meant to reflect the character and nature of our Creator to the world. Through redemption in Jesus and a heart transformed by grace, truth, and the Holy Spirit, we can glorify our heavenly Father. God created us for His glory.[2] It's what we were designed to do.

The brother of Jesus (James), under the inspiration of the Holy Spirit, drew a conclusion about what it means to have a pure religion. He said, "Religion that is pure and undefiled before God the Father is this: to visit orphans and widows in their affliction, and to keep oneself unstained from the world" (James 1:27). How we treat those who seem to have nothing to offer us says a lot about our relationship with God. We show what we believe by what we do. Pure religion flows from a recognition that we were once far from God yet known by God. And now, we are called to care for those who need to know God and see the light of the gospel of Christ.

My mom worked for a time at a high-end jewelry store. Luckily for me, when it came time to propose, I had a friend in the diamond business. Unfortunately, I knew nothing about diamonds. My mom took the time to explain to me the 4 C's of diamonds—cut, color, clarity, and carat. While leaning over that glass counter, she would hand me a ring with a modest diamond, and then a little one-eye microscope called a loupe. Through this loupe, I could see what the diamond was really made of. What looked to be a perfect diamond from my naked eye would turn out to have tiny dark flecks throughout. I looked through dozens of rings and eventually picked out the best one that fit my budget. Thankfully, April did say yes. I still think my cool red hat from the night we met had something to do with that.

If we want to look into our hearts and see what our devotion to Jesus truly looks like, the loupe we should use is one of love without expectation. If we look through that loupe—how we treat those who don't have anything to offer in return—what would we see? We should see a heart that is willing to see others. The best indicator of the posture of our heart wouldn't be our attitude toward a big client or donor. We wouldn't examine how we treat a supervisor, teacher, or coach who we're trying to impress. Rather, how do we treat the broken, challenging, and lonely?

Bought by Jesus—Saved by and for Grace

God has a beautiful design for the world. We were made to live in harmony in our relationship with God, ourselves, others, and God's created world. Instead of living perfectly in His design, we turn and go our own way. The Bible has a word for this act of turning away—sin. Wayne Grudem defines sin this way: "Sin is any failure to conform to the moral law of God in act, attitude, or nature."[3]

Sin leads to brokenness in our lives and brokenness in our world. Where God intends richness and significance in our relationships, we often only see the brokenness of sin. This brokenness leads people to try and find a way out of the brokenness they feel. Addiction, money, and social status initially ease the pain of brokenness, but in the end we feel empty once again. There is only one thing that can heal the brokenness we see in the world—the gospel.

The gospel is the life, death, burial, and resurrection of Jesus. Paul says in 1 Corinthians 15:1–7 (CSB):

> Now I want to make clear for you, brothers
> and sisters, the gospel I preached to you,
> which you received, on which you have taken
> your stand and by which you are being saved,
> if you hold to the message I preached to you—
> unless you believed in vain. For I passed on to
> you as most important what I also received:
> that Christ died for our sins according to
> the Scriptures, that he was buried, that he
> was raised on the third day according to the
> Scriptures, and that he appeared to Cephas,
> then to the Twelve. Then he appeared to over
> five hundred brothers and sisters at one time;
> most of them are still alive, but some have
> fallen asleep. Then he appeared to James, then
> to all the apostles.

Paul made the gospel clear. He was intent on spelling out exactly what the gospel is because he knew his audience had a tendency to get things confused or misinterpret them. Paul reminded them. We feel the urge to remind people of things when we perceive that they may forget. My wife often reminds me to return items to Home Depot, pick up the kids from practice, and clean the floors before guests arrive. She reminds because she perceives I might forget. We are reminded of the gospel by the Holy Spirit through the apostle Paul because of our tendency to forget.

Today, we lack clarity about the gospel. At its core, the word "gospel" simply means "good news." Have you ever received good news? The words, "It's a girl!" or "You're cancer free!" can ignite in us a celebratory feeling like no other. The gospel is good news even better than the examples I just offered. A gospel message in New Testament times was a declaration of victory. The victory of the gospel is a proclamation that Jesus has defeated sin, sickness, and death in His life, death, burial, and resurrection. Best of all, Jesus invites us into His victory.

Paul made this gospel message abundantly clear. He wants to make clear who Jesus is and what He came to do so that Christians would have no uncertainty or confusion about His purpose. In fact, Paul says that this gospel is "most important." The gospel is not *a* thing in Christianity. The gospel is *the* thing in Christianity. J. D. Greear often says that the gospel is not just the diving board that gets you into the pool of Christianity. The gospel is the pool itself.[4]

The good news of Christianity centers on the life, death, burial, and resurrection of Jesus. Jesus lived a perfect life (unlike our sinful life). He died an excruciating death on a cross. His body was broken, His blood was shed, and the heart in His body stopped beating. Jesus was buried, rose victorious from the grave, and is actively at work in the world today through the power of the Holy Spirit.

The good news makes transformation possible. We don't have to aimlessly bump through life from one pleasure or unmet expectation to another. Our heavenly Father saved us, and is saving us, through our belief and repentance. We are set free from our own desires to live a life of purpose. Augustine, in his book *Confessions*, recounts, "You have made us for yourself, and our hearts are restless until they find their rest in you."[5] Transformed by the Spirit and the message of the gospel, we are counter-surfing pleasure seekers. We are set free to love, share, give, and see others.

Let's be real. In many areas of our country, there is a church on almost every corner. There are more denominations than we have fingers and toes to count them on. We have church on TV, the internet, and even on social media. One may think that with all of the religion among us, we would be overflowing with kindness. We may conclude that we don't need a book about seeing people. However, what we often see is a monumental disconnect between the grace we are shown by God and the grace we show others. Ray Ortlund says it this way:

> The gospel says something and the gospel does something. The gospel says the truths of Christ crucified, buried, risen again, and returning. What the gospel does through what it says is create beauty in human relationships. The vertical glories of the gospel come down upon us in a church and spread out horizontally.[6]

Every one of us wants to see beauty in human relationships. Perhaps you had an earthly father who didn't quite show you the love you always wanted. Maybe you look back on your school days and remember wanting just one good friend, who truly knew you and was with you every step of the way. Perhaps even today you desire that same type of friendship that you've longed for. You want to know and be known in an extraordinary way. God created us for beautiful relationships. He desires for us to flourish. Yet in brokenness we often don't see the type of connections we were designed for.

What if we gently and graciously stepped into the lives of others? What if those around us knew that we were that one person they could trust with the most challenging secrets of their life? What if we actually believed the radically counter-cultural idea that we could hear of the brokenness in others' lives and stay at the table with them nonetheless. So much is at stake. The most convincing proof of the truth and power of the gospel will not come from well-crafted arguments alone, but rather from our radiant kindness. Are we willing to put ourselves out there? Can we overlook offense, move beyond our own selfish desires, and focus on the precious image-bearers around us each day? And if not, then why not?

I'm not a doomsday church guy. I can't bring myself to say things like, "We may lose the faith and the church if we don't pass it on to the next generation." I believe Jesus when He said that the gates of hell will not prevail against the church. Nothing can stop the mission of God. However, I do think the next generation is watching. The next generation will find faith more difficult not because they don't believe what the church teaches, but because they believe the church itself doesn't believe what the church teaches.[7]

I have lots of friends who have been introduced to CrossFit. I didn't intend for this book to be controversial, so I hesitate to bring up such a divisive topic as CrossFit. Many people

imagine CrossFit as only tremendously fit individuals flip-
ping tires, doing weird pull-ups, and grunting while lifting
barbells loaded to the brim. Some conclude that they'd have
to get in shape in order to start working out alongside the fit
individuals they see in their mind. They tell me they would feel
embarrassed jumping into a class, imagining they would fail
miserably in a pool of sweat and tears. They think they have to
get in shape before they start.

Sadly, many believe a similar falsehood when it comes to
drawing near to Jesus (and maybe to us). They imagine they'd
need to clean themselves up in order for Jesus to accept them.
This couldn't be further from the truth. People need to see a
living gospel in us where we draw near to others not based on
their usefulness to us, their moral scorecard, or their sharing
of our worldview. As our heavenly Father has been to us, so
may we be to others.

I don't enjoy many songs from the 1700s, but one that I do
love is "Come, Ye Sinners, Poor and Needy." They don't name
songs like that anymore. One particular line in the song drives
deep to the middle of my heart every time I hear it:

> Come, ye weary, heavy-laden,
> Lost and ruined by the fall;
> If you tarry till you're better,
> You will never come at all.

We all have burdens. At times, we're even "heavy-laden."
We live under emotional, mental, and spiritual fatigue. We're
hopeless without Christ. But if we tarry (wait) until we're

cleaned up, we'll never come to Jesus at all. Jesus does not call us to wait. We are called to draw near to God, through the broken body and shed blood of Jesus, in full assurance of faith (Hebrews 10). It's as though our Lord calls us to walk right into His office whenever we please. Through the righteousness of Christ, our heavenly Father has an open-door policy, and He loves to have us near.

If you're the kind of person that feels unworthy of the presence of God, you're at the perfect place to draw near in His presence. We don't deserve His love, yet He gave it extravagantly to us in the person and work of Jesus. In Ephesians 1, we see that Jesus lavishes three things on us: redemption, forgiveness, and grace:

> In him we have redemption through his blood,
> the forgiveness of our trespasses, according to
> the riches of his grace, which he lavished upon
> us, in all wisdom and insight. (vv. 7–8)

Jesus didn't just help us squeak by. He lavishes His graces on us. This word *lavish* means to go over and above, or to give in abundance. It's way more than we could ever need.

Every year at Thanksgiving, my wife's grandmother makes about ten times more food than we could all possibly eat. Her Thanksgiving table could handle a platoon of 100 hungry soldiers and still have 9.4 turkeys to spare. She goes overboard. And it's awesome—in part because of the leftovers. I can't remember a Thanksgiving that we didn't go home without an armful of plastic bags. We'd walk away with stuffing, turkey, gravy, rolls, and cranberry sauce—all in abundance. It would be humanly impossible for us to eat everything she would give us, yet she would give it to us nonetheless.

Our heavenly Father does the same. Through our belief and repentance, our heavenly Father lavishes grace on us. This is grace upon grace upon grace. Lamentations 3:22–23 tell us that:

> The steadfast love of the LORD never ceases;
> his mercies never come to an end; they are
> new every morning; great is your faithfulness.

When I open my eyes in the morning, there is new mercy that the Lord has prepared for me. When my feet hit the floor and I stand up, there is the Lord, placing too many plastic bags of grace in my arms. This grace is more than sufficient for the challenges from within and all around me. Our only claim to the presence of God is the righteousness of Jesus offered to us on the cross. We didn't earn it, and we could never pay the Lord back.

Alistair Begg is a hero of mine. He has served as the senior pastor of Cleveland's Parkside Church since 1983, and he is also the voice behind the *Truth for Life* Christian radio preaching and teaching ministry. Alistair once preached a sermon titled "The Power and Message of the Cross." In this message, Alistair masterfully paints the picture of Jesus on the cross flanked by two criminals. The preacher goes on to share that it would be a sight to meet that one criminal who turned to Jesus when he arrived in glory. The criminal had never been to a Bible study. He hadn't been baptized to profess his faith. He didn't have all the answers. The criminal, imagines Alistair, might be asked by angels, "What are you doing here?" To which he would reply, "I don't know." Maybe the angels would ask, "What do you mean you don't know?" The criminal would reply, "I mean I don't know!"

The angels would then shuffle around in discussion and confusion and then go get their supervisor. The supervisor might then ask, "Are you clear on the major doctrines?" "No," the criminal would reply. "Do you understand the doctrine of justification by faith?" the angel would ask. "No, sorry," the criminal would reply. The angel, in frustration, would ask one final question: "Okay then, on what basis are you here?" The criminal replies, "The man on the middle cross said I could come." Alistair concludes, "That is the only correct answer to that question."[8] If Jesus is our only answer, then why would we withhold grace from the valuable, amazing image-bearers around us each day?

The Big Hinge Point

If our heavenly Father poured out grace on us, then how can we not pour out grace on those around us? What could be keeping us from showing that same grace to a world that desperately needs to know it? With our countenance, tone, and reaction to others, do we set an unspoken expectation that people need to have it all together in order for us to draw near to them?

The apostle Peter once asked Jesus how many times we should forgive a person who sins against us. It's likely that Peter was looking for a way to not forgive someone who had wronged him. In essence, Peter's question was, "How long do I have to put up with the people around me?" Jesus told Peter that he should forgive others seventy times seven. Quick math would tell us that the answer was 490 times. But Jesus wasn't doing quick math. Jesus's answer revealed to Peter that we should forgive again, and again, and again, and again.

Jesus went on to tell the story of a king who decided to call his debts from his borrowers. One debtor was brought in who owed millions of dollars, which the debtor did not have. The king then instructed the man to take extreme measures, selling himself and his entire family in order to repay the debt. The debtor fell to his knees and begged the king to be patient with him. Matthew 18:27 reveals that, "out of pity for him, the master of that servant released him and forgave him the debt." The debtor owed a debt he could not repay, but he walked away not owing a single penny.

However, not long after leaving the king's presence, the debtor went to a fellow servant who owed him just a few thousand dollars. The man who had just been forgiven refused to forgive, grabbing his fellow servant by the throat and demanding payment. Even after his debtor begged him, just as he had begged the king, he refused. Despite the borrower's pleading, he had his debtor thrown in prison. Onlookers witnessed the man roughing up his debtor, even though he had been forgiven much, and they went to the king to recount the whole experience.

As you could imagine, the king was furious. He called in the man and said, "'You evil servant! I forgave you that tremendous debt because you pleaded with me. Shouldn't you have mercy on your fellow servant, just as I had mercy on you?' Then the angry king sent the man to prison to be tortured until he had paid his entire debt" (Matt. 18:32–34 NLT). He had been forgiven millions, but couldn't let go of a few thousand. Jesus added this warning: "That's what my heavenly Father will do to you if you refuse to forgive your brothers and sisters from your heart" (v. 35 NLT).

We are called to view others through the lens of grace. Grace shown to us is supposed to go through us. Even when others wrong us, Jesus calls us to offer love and mercy. Our culture often chants for revenge, saying we ought to give others what they deserve. But the gospel story is different. We've been shown good news that sets us free from our debt of sin. We're then called to reflect that grace to the image-bearers around us.

As a pastor, I attend a lot of funerals. I've noticed something very odd about these events. We often save the nicest things to say about a person for the event held after they're gone. Friends and family members one after another often say the most beautiful remarks in memory of their loved one. I would venture to guess that the people who walk, drive, and run past us each day would be encouraged by the unsaid thoughts of the people around them. What if instead of waiting for a wedding speech, a 40th birthday party, or heaven forbid a funeral, we took the time to speak wonderful words of encouragement, value, and love over those around us?

Why do we often define others by their worst moments? Why do we allow a single conversation, or one act on their part, or catching them in a moment of anger to define everything about them? One reason may be because we don't yet know the best thing about them. It's easier (and dare I say more prideful) to define others by their worst moments. We're enraged at the thought that others would do the same to us.

The grace of Jesus flowing through our souls must lead us to show others, "I see you in your pain." The grace of Jesus leads us beyond our own interests and toward the interests of others. Philippians 2:4 admonishes us to "let each of you look not only to his own interests, but also to the interests of others." We can see people who we don't agree with. We can see people who don't look like us. We can even see people who mistreat us. In fact, Jesus Matthew 5 tells us we are the ones who are blessed if people insult us for the love that we have in Christ.

Francis Shaeffer was a brilliant American evangelical theologian, philosopher, and Presbyterian pastor. He wrote numerous books and preached hundreds, if not thousands, of sermons. After Shaeffer's death, his followers compiled a collection of sermons all centered on one theme in his preaching. While Shaeffer often wrote in dense theological and philosophical terms, this collection of sermons reinforced a central theme of Shaeffer's conclusions. The result was a book with a title that rightly encompasses the theme of the messages—*No Little People*. While Shaeffer was orthodox in his doctrine, he also put forth a right practice in our tone and attitude toward others—there are no little people. We are valuable, magnificent creations of our heavenly Father, and we must treat others with the amazing value inherent in those who bear the image of their Creator.

• Reflection Questions •

1. What is your most valuable possession? Why is it valuable to you?

2. How do people in our culture tend to measure their value? The value of others?

3. How is our culture's view of human value different than what we see in Genesis 1?

4. Why do we often have a disconnect between the grace shown to us by God and the grace we show to others?

5. How might we, or our church, inadvertently send the message that people must clean themselves up before they can draw near?

6. How does the gospel message open up our lives to others?

7. Would you be willing to confess to the Lord (and perhaps to others) that you struggle to value people around you? Would you ask the Lord to change your heart?

4

FOCUS

*If we are to love our neighbors, before doing
anything else, we must see our neighbors. With
our imagination as well as our eyes, that is to
say like artists, we must see not just their faces
but the life behind and within their faces. Here
it is love that is the frame we see them in.*[1]
—Frederick Buechner

On a recent trip to New York City with my family, I was determined for everyone to see Van Gogh's painting *The Starry
Night*. Early one morning, we ventured out of our brownstone
Airbnb in Harlem and set out for the Metropolitan Museum
of Art. We walked several blocks to the subway station, rode
the 5 train, and then walked several more blocks up to the
museum. We stood outside for a moment, just staring at the
Met, a marvelous building that's welcomed visitors since 1872.
We walked up those iconic stone steps, through the massive
doors, and into the grand foyer. In my polite, Southern-ish
accent, I approached a staff member at the welcome desk and
asked, "Can you show me on this map where we can find *The
Starry Night*? The staff member looked me in the eyes and
replied, "What you are going to want to do is turn around, go

right back out those front doors, and walk to the Museum of Modern Art. That's where you'll find it."

Needless to say, we didn't see the painting that day, but I still think it's an interesting piece of art. As with most pieces of art, we like to ask the question, "What is this painting about?" Some may say it's exactly what it's titled: a painting of a night sky, with swirls of color and dashes of moonlight. The painting also seems to depict a large cypress, a village, hills, hay bales, and even a church. For centuries, people have wondered about the meaning beyond the physical elements of the painting. Van Gogh made references in his writing to a world beyond death, and he often used imagery of the sky to depict what is to come. Perhaps the image of a night sky calmed him by bringing his mind to eternity.

We often see Van Gogh as a brilliant artist—after all, he is one of the most famous painters in the world. But many don't know the story of the man behind the art. Van Gogh was born into a long line of Dutch Reformed pastors, and even trained to become a pastor himself. When he was rejected from the ministry, he began his own outreach, living among the poor and oppressed in meager conditions. Ministry leaders later rejected Van Gogh, calling him unfit for the dignity of the priesthood. Van Gogh was not without troubles himself, and in the aftermath of self-mutilation, he voluntarily admitted himself to the Saint-Rémy-de-Provence mental asylum on May 8, 1889. It was from this asylum that he painted this famous work. *The Starry Night* isn't just a famous painting. It's a visual symphony of sky, stars, moon, a village, and a church—and the man behind the brushstrokes.

As we journeyed through the Metropolitan Museum of Art, I noticed small benches in front of key works of art. My children trotted quickly from room to room, but I saw others sit down to take in individual works seeking to experience the totality of each piece. I saw a couple sit in front of Pollock's *Autumn Rhythm (Number 30)* for twenty minutes, conversing about the coordination and chaos of the paint drippings and splashes.

Every person we encounter is like a painting. We can glance by quickly and classify someone as a coach, wife, attorney, teacher, coworker, or Uber driver, just like many classify Van Gogh's work as a picture of the sky at night. But upon closer examination, we are all more than simple titles or categories of people. We are fully human, a divinely created composition of many elements that make us who we are. We have a past, dreams, hopes, and pains. We have a story. And we all want someone to see us. We're more than the individual brushstroke moments of our life. Our whole life paints a bigger picture.

The Difference Is Focus

The difference between glancing through a crowd and meaningfully connecting with people is *focus*. Jesus often found Himself in a crowd. Interested onlookers, skeptics, devotees, and even a traitor kept company with Jesus. But Jesus didn't see just a crowd. He saw individual people.

Luke 19 introduces us to a man in Jericho named Zacchaeus who desperately wanted to see Jesus. Zacchaeus's life reflected many of the characteristics others would deem important. He was rich, powerful, and well-connected. As goods moved along the travel route in Jericho, Zacchaeus was right there, collecting taxes from the traders. Though they were wealthy, tax collectors (especially chief tax collectors like Zacchaeus) were despised in their communities. But at this point in his life, Zacchaeus had learned that riches and notoriety don't satisfy the deepest longings of our hearts. He wanted salvation, and he'd do anything to get it. That's when Jesus showed up, walking the path from Jerusalem to Jericho.

Zacchaeus was short, so he couldn't see above the crowds. I imagine him walking behind the crowds, leaping to glance above shoulders with coins jingling in his bag. Determined, Zacchaeus climbed a tree to get a better view of Jesus. Tree climbing would never have appeared on a list of dignified activities in first-century Palestine, but Zacchaeus wasn't going to let society's rules keep him from a view of Jesus.

Jesus saw Zacchaeus and even knew his name. Perhaps this was a supernatural act, or maybe Jesus just happened to notice a grown man in a tree. Regardless, Jesus saw him and called out, "Hurry, come down here. I'd like to come and stay at your house." That simple statement puts magnificent grace on display. Jesus didn't receive this hated man with disdain, disgust, or dismay. Instead, Jesus received him *joyfully*. Imagine the face of Jesus smiling, maybe even laughing, as Zacchaeus walked toward His outstretched arms of embrace. This is precisely what it means to focus.

Others in the crowd grumbled that Jesus would associate with a sinner like Zacchaeus. But at dinner, Zacchaeus showed the true nature of his heart, offering to give away half of his entire fortune and even pay back fourfold anyone he had cheated. Jesus, in response, said, "Today salvation has come to this house, since he also is a son of Abraham. For the Son of Man came to seek and to save the lost" (Luke 19:9–10). The affection of Jesus drew in the most hated man in town and changed his heart.

A. W. Tozer said, "What comes into our minds when we think about God is the most important thing about us."[2] I remember a story of a young woman who said she thought of Jesus as the sum total of all the Christians she had ever met. After pondering this Jesus, she concluded that she and this Jesus probably wouldn't like each other very much. I wish she could see the true face of Jesus, the one Zacchaeus saw.

Have you thought specifically enough about Jesus to ponder the fact that Jesus had eyes? Although we don't know the color of His eyes, we can imagine the nature of them. Eyes tell a lot about a person. We notice a young person locked into the draw of scrolling on their phone. We'll never forget the eyes of a mother at the sight of a child's obstinance. There were times when Jesus was righteously angry, and those eyes told a story. Often, Jesus drew into the circumstances of a person who reached out toward Him. I envision Christ's eye contact was such that didn't intimidate but communicated power. My imagination takes me to eyes that were undistracted, focused, full of overwhelming and compelling grace.

The human eye is a marvel. The eye is one of the most complex parts of the body, second only to the brain. Although it takes up just .025 percent of our body weight, it processes 80 percent of the information that we receive. The eye has 137 million special cells that respond to light, 130 million cells that respond to black and white, and 7 million cells that respond to color. The optic nerve sends signals from our eyes to our brain, and the brain converts those signals into usable information. The eye, optical nerve, and visual cortex capture and deliver 5.4 trillion messages per hour. If the eye was a digital camera, it would be 576 megapixels. The main camera in the most current iPhone is only 48 megapixels.[3]

What's even more fascinating is that we all process what we see in an entirely different way. Don't believe me? Think about those little wrinkly dogs called pugs. One person may say, "A pug is like a bundle of love gift-wrapped in fur!" while another says, "The pug is living proof that God has a sense of humor." Do a simple Google search and you'll find pug puppies in tea cups, pugs in tutus, and even pictures depicting Jesus holding a pug (not sure about that one). Some find pugs to be beautiful. Others, not so much.

My neighbor and I can view the same thing but see something altogether different. In your workplace, you may see cubicles filled with coworkers, or rectangles on Zoom with salespeople from another region. You could also look more closely and see Ellie, the single mom doing her best in the workplace while taking care of her two children, or Tom, who spends his weekends caring for his aging parents. Just because we have sight doesn't necessarily mean that we will see the same thing. Seeing people the way Jesus saw people requires focus. Mary Schaller and John Crilly call this "The Art of Noticing." They define *noticing* as "The spiritual discipline of intentionally paying attention to someone who is in your view at the moment, wherever you are."[4]

I'm proposing that by the power of the Holy Spirit and responding to the message of the gospel that we can change the way we see and think about others. We can choose how we think. Right now, if you choose to draw a picture in your mind of a pink elephant balancing itself on a ball, you can. You chose that thought. Even if you chose *not* to think of the elephant (and maybe by now you can't think of anything else), you chose to think of something else. We have to quit seeing our thoughts and feelings as a cage and start seeing them as a tool, and a tool that we can wield for the glory of Jesus.

Learn to Observe

Tim Tebow made headlines as a standout high school football player in the state of Florida. He went on to play for Urban Meyer at the University of Florida, won a Heisman trophy, and led his team to two national championships. I'll never forget the 2008 post-game promise Tim made after the Ole Miss Rebels upset Florida 31–30. Fighting back tears, Tebow vowed that no one would work harder than he and his teammates the rest of the year. The Gators responded by going undefeated for the rest of the season and beating Oklahoma 24–14 to win their second national title in three years.

I had the opportunity to be a part of two different month-long mission trips with the Tebow family. As awesome as Tim may be, I found his mom and dad to be even more so. Pam Tebow is a gentle and warm presence with an endearing smile. The day I met Pam, she asked me about my family, children, and ministry. She is the kind of person that you'll have a hard time getting to talk about herself. Bob Tebow is a mountain of a person, both in his confidence in Christ and his care for others. At one moment, Bob will be getting others to sing and dance along with him, and in the next moment he'll be preaching with power from the truth of the Bible.

I once asked Bob to advise me, a young pastor at the time, about how to be the best preacher that I could be. I think Bob's answer will help all of us who want to see people the way Jesus saw people. Bob responded quickly with one word, "observation." He went on to explain that the most effective ministers are people who have developed the skill of observation. First, they observe the Bible to understand God's truth to us. He said that we should observe God's Word well and often. We can't skimp in our study of the Scriptures. Then, Bob reminded me to observe myself, learning to be effective with my strengths and my weaknesses.

Lastly, Bob advised me to observe others. When we communicate the gospel *to* people, let's not forget that we are communicating *with* people. The people around us have personal victories, struggles, hang ups, and challenges. Every person is different. If we don't observe the people to whom we speak, we become irrelevant, or worse, without love. The apostle Paul said it like this in 1 Corinthians 13:1–3:

> If I speak in the tongues of men and of angels, but have not love, I am a noisy gong or a clanging cymbal. And if I have prophetic powers, and understand all mysteries and all knowledge, and if I have all faith, so as to remove mountains, but have not love, I am nothing. If I give away all I have, and if I deliver up my body to be burned, but have not love, I gain nothing.

Reduce Distractions

The opposite of focus is distraction, and our culture is more distracted than any other time in history. Nicholas Carr, author of *The Shadows: What the Internet Is Doing to Our Brains*, says, "What the Net seems to be doing is chipping away my capacity for concentration and contemplation. Whether I'm online or not, my mind now expects to take in information the way the Net distributes it: in a swiftly moving stream of particles. Once I was a scuba diver in the sea of words. Now I zip along the surface like a guy on a Jet Ski."[5] It's like Nicholas has a front-row seat to see inside my thoughts.

Carr wrote this book in 2011 as the iPhone 4s was released, ushering in a whole new slate of features. At the time I'm writing this book, there have been 34 more updated versions of the iPhone, 22 more iterations of the iPad, 5G speeds, and widespread gigabit speed internet. Patricia Greenfield concluded that "every medium develops some cognitive skills at the expense of others."[6] Our attraction to our devices may be at the expense of practicing presence with others.

The Insider reports that screen time continues to go up as well. In the United States, children between the ages of eight and twelve spend an average of 4 to 6 hours per day looking at screens, and teens may spend as much as 9 hours per day. Contrary to popular belief, adults spend even more time on screens—on average, just over 10.5 hours each day.[7] If we spend an average of 8 hours each night asleep, that leaves just 5.5 hours that we could be physically present and focused with others. The Roman philosopher Seneca said this 2,000 years ago: "To be everywhere is to be nowhere."

We're more connected than ever, but we may not be happier. A large study in 2018 (using data from more than 40,000 two- to seventeen-year-old children and adolescents in the U.S.) concluded that among fourteen- to seventeen-year-olds, high users of screens (7+ hours per day vs. low users of 1 hour per day) were more than twice as likely to have been diagnosed with depression. According to a recent survey by Cigna, 61 percent of Americans are lonely, with an increasing number of people reporting feeling like they are left out, poorly understood, and lacking companionship.[8] Cigna also found a nearly

13 percent rise in loneliness since 2018. Doug Nemecek, chief medical officer for behavioral health at Cigna, concluded, "In-person connections are what really matters. Sharing that time to have a meaningful interaction and a meaningful conversation, to share our lives with others, is important to help us mitigate and minimize loneliness."[9]

The more we increase our screen time—thereby increasing rates of distraction, loneliness, and depression—the more precious a resource focus becomes. When we believe something is valuable and rare, we'll fight for it, protect it, save it, and even savor it. As we see in the life of Jesus, focusing on the lives of others is like gold. Envision how your home, workplace, barber shop, gym, or neighborhood would transform if you treasured intentional presence with others. The Survey Center on American Life revealed that in 1995, 3 percent of American men reported that they did not have a single friend. In 2021, the number rose to 15 percent. In 1995, 59 percent of American men said they had 6 good friends. In 2021, the number plummeted to 27 percent.[10] I'm not saying that screens are all to blame, but I am saying they likely aren't helping.

In the 1970s, it was reported that an average person saw between 500 and 1,600 ads per day.[11] Before our digital age, advertisements could be found on billboards, in newspapers, and on TV shows and commercials promoting the latest products and services. The market research firm Yankelovich estimated that by 2007, the average person saw up to 5,000 ads per day.[12] While many would say that the amount of advertising at this time was out of control, one product, introduced in 2007, would take advertising saturation into the stratosphere—the iPhone. Today, with tiny computers in our pockets, the average person encounters between 6,000 and 10,000 ads every single day.

These ads are filled with the message that what we have and who we are not sufficient. We need their product or service to fix our deficiencies. They tell us we need clothes, technology, cars, houses, and weight-loss programs. And they'll do it thousands of times each day. For a world that's already wrought with anxiety, fear, and worry, what if we were radically present as a steady, kind, gentle, and warm anchor to show them, with our lips and our lives, that they are valued?

We are drawn toward what we value. Our interests catch our eye. Advertisers leverage our follower list on social media for the opportunity to target our interests with well-placed advertisements. If you follow people in the culinary world, you may see ads for cookware and cutlery. If you follow athletes from the NBA, you'll see ads for tickets or basketball apparel. Our eye notices what we value. Humanity is the crown jewel of God's creation. God made all things and said they were good. But when God created people, He said we are "very good." Through prayer, intentionality, and the Holy Spirit, we can experience transformation in what we value. Jesus can move our eyes to "catch" on the people around us. Paul wrote to the church at Thessalonica, "So, being affectionately desirous of you, we were ready to share with you not only the gospel of God but also our own selves, because you had become very dear to us" (1 Thess. 2:8).

Focus is now a superpower. While most everyone else is distracted, we can be the rare exception. We don't have to be slaves to our phones, or our worries, or our own pleasure. We're set free by the gospel of Christ. The Holy Spirit of God lives inside of those who turn to Him. We have the opportunity to be the rare exception. Simply drawing our eyes to one person at a time and showing with our demeanor, eyes, and smile that people matter put us at another level in our work, influence, and most importantly, our gospel conversations.

Bob Goff tells the story of his friend Randy, who was instrumental in leading Bob closer to Jesus. Goff says of Randy, "He didn't just say he was for me or with me. He was actually present with me."[13] When he saw Bob attempt to drop out of high school, Randy made the choice, just days after his own wedding, to set out on a road trip adventure with Bob. It was through this radical, abundant, over-the-top presence that Bob felt loved, accepted, and cared for. Goff reflects on his adventure with Randy: "But the kind of love that God created and demonstrated is a costly one because it involves sacrifice and presence. It's a love that operates more like a sign language than being spoken outright. What I learned from Randy about the brand of love Jesus offers is that it's more about presence than undertaking a project. It's a brand of love that doesn't just think about good things, or agree with them, or talk about them."

Practical Ways to Block Distractions

Be fully present

We all communicate nonverbally. In fact, studies have shown that 60 to 80 percent of our communication is nonverbal. Our eye contact, shoulder position, facial expressions, and posture all communicate just as strongly as the words coming out of our mouths. We can tell someone that we care and we value them by the physical presence we exude. I have a friend who told me that he recently became aware that the way he sits in meetings communicates a spirit of overconfidence and dominance. He had no idea. Now he can consciously make an effort to ensure that his posture is not communicating an attitude he doesn't wish to convey. Your laptop may be essential in meetings, but what if it sits off to the side a bit, communicating even more that you're present in the meeting?

When we first begin to practice intentional presence, we will probably find the process to be difficult. In order to focus on others, we need to step back and reassess the quantity and quality of our media consumption. Romans 12:2 tells us, "Do not be conformed to this world, but be transformed by the renewal of your mind, that by testing you may discern what is the will of God, what is good and acceptable and perfect." If we want the will of God for our lives, which is good and acceptable and perfect, we have to commit to a renewal of our minds. We may need accountability from others and new routines in order to break our habits.

Do you know someone who can make you feel as though you're the only person in their life in that moment? If we want to see people, our eyes will tell a story. It may be a difficult practice to remain visually present with a person, but it's worth it. I'm not talking about giving our neighbors a creepy stare. What I *am* encouraging is a presence that communicates to another person, "You are valuable to me—more valuable than my phone, my next appointment, or the environment around us." Our eyes, shoulders, and posture all communicate something.

Here are a few questions you can ask others to assess your self-awareness and presence with others:

"Do you feel like I'm fully present when I'm in a conversation with you?"

"How do you think people perceive me in meetings?"

"What can I do to better communicate with my team, family, or with you that you are valuable to me?"

"What do I do too much of that keeps me from creating deeper connections with others?"

"What do I do too little of that keeps me from creating deeper connections with others?"

Ask better questions, listen well, and talk less. "How are you doing, really?" This question cuts through mere pleasantries and drives to the core of what's happening in our hearts. While men in particular may be afraid to share feelings, I believe deep down we do want to be known and know others. God made us this way. "How are you doing, really?" is an invitation for a person to share something deeper, and a call for us to truly listen.

Freelance graphic design helped me pay my way through my master's degree. I wasn't much of an artist, but I did understand graphic design software and could follow instructions from clients. One of the early design lessons I learned was the importance of negative space. Negative space is the space between elements of a design and around the main subject. I often tried to fill as much "cool" as I could into a business card, flyer, logo, or booklet. That caused the end product to look jumbled and crowded. Learning to incorporate empty space made a huge difference in my design. Sometimes, less is better.

Often, "I'm sorry" is the most appropriate response. We can also ask good questions such as "How did you feel?" or "How did you respond?" or "What's the hardest part about all of that?" The best conversationalists aren't people who keep the wheel spinning with astounding stories. The best conversationalists ask good questions. When we speak less and listen more, we create space for others to feel heard.

One of my mentors, Jimmy Scroggins, is excellent at creating space in conversations. My wife and I often joke about Jimmy's ability to look into your soul during a conversation. He asks excellent questions that move me to inspect my motives and articulate my conclusions. Jimmy's influence in my life has come not only from the wisdom he has shared with me, but also from the fantastic questions he asks and the posture from which he listens. A simple "What are you hoping that will accomplish?" or "Why would you want to do that?" has changed the course of several decisions in my life.

Ask good questions, but stay focused as an answer comes. Really listening is a gift. James gives a reminder that we all need: "Know this, my beloved brothers: let every person be quick to hear, slow to speak, slow to anger" (James 1:19). I'm often quick to speak, slow to listen, and continually ask the Lord to make me a better listener. I don't always have to give advice or say a perfect word. Proverbs 18:2 tells us, "A fool takes no pleasure in understanding, but only in expressing his opinion." Want to listen better? Step one: talk less.

One illustration of the importance of listening more and talking less is found in a popular meme that made its way around social media. You may be familiar with the image of a bearded man holding a cup of coffee with a fake half smile. It's interesting how such simple pictures can be so widely representative of our emotions. The caption of this particular meme, in reference to this fake half smile, reads, "When you're 10 dangs, 20 yups, 6 wows, and 8 man that's crazy's, and they still won't stop talking." Funny. The first step in listening better may be gaining self-awareness that we talk exponentially more than others would like to hear.

Serve the moment

My dad is hilarious. He has a quick wit that can lighten the mood in almost any circumstance. I often try to be like my father, inserting a witty quip into my conversations. My friend Nathan once told me, "You know, you don't have to always try to be funny." I'm glad he corrected me and reminded me to show up as my real self. There's nothing inherently wrong with humor, but I've often found myself listening for the intent of approval of others in the form of a laugh rather than seeking to truly listen to what others are saying. People are not a means to fill my own craving for approval. People are valuable image-bearers of God.

Asking myself, "How can I serve the moment?" also keeps me from talking all about myself. It can be good to share personal experiences and observations from time to time, but we've all met someone who comedian Brian Regan affectionately calls a "Me Monster."[14] Practicing the discipline of listening for the good of others may be exhausting at first. Listening well is like a muscle, and muscles are built over time with repetitions. We can coach our employees, children, and one another with a simple question: "Do you feel like you best served the moment?"

My friend Chris (more on him later) talks about seeing people past, present, and future. Admittedly, Chris is best about seeing people for their own future. He asks people questions about where they want to go, what they want to do, and who they want to be. Chris's wife, Lyndie, is much better at seeing people in the present. She can meet someone in their current circumstances and listen with purpose. Others are best at seeing people in their past, asking great questions about what makes a person who they are. We can see people in conversation, past, present, and future. Doug Pollock writes in his book *God Space*, "Noticing is a prerequisite to caring about others and serving them in tangible ways that smuggle the gospel into their hearts."[15]

What Do We Do If Van Gogh Is Right?

The view outside Van Gogh's asylum window did not include a church, but in *The Starry Night*, we find a darkened church building. Though easily missed, it's actually key to the overall composition of the painting. Along with the giant cypress, it is the only vertical form, breaking the mostly horizontal construction of the work. Artist Makoto Fujimura reflects, "The cypress tree and the church are two forms that connect heaven and earth. Without the church, the cypress tree takes over the swirl of movement, and there's no visual center to hold the painting in tension between heaven and earth."[16]

On closer examination, we see that the church is the only building in the town without lights. Several scholars postulate that Van Gogh painted the dark church as a statement that the Spirit has left the church, or at least the building. Fujimura goes on to ask, "The church has kept the structure of the Truth in society, but we have lost the Spirit in creating beauty. . . .

What do we do if Vincent is right; what do we do in a culture in which the light of the Spirit has gone out of the church buildings and instead went swirling into Nature and into the margins of the life?"[17]

Van Gogh would have just three full years devoted to painting. The artist did not eat properly and often drank heavily. He was commercially unsuccessful in his lifetime, and many regarded him as a madman and a failure.[18] On July 27, 1890, Van Gogh shot himself in the chest at the age of thirty-seven. Two days later he passed away. The artist's brother, Theo, reported that Van Gogh's last words were, "The sadness will last forever."[19]

It's time for us to take the light to a world plagued by darkness. We must be the ones who march forward with the message of hope. Proverbs 4:19 says of those who walk in darkness, "They do not know over what they stumble." How many people around us each day are stumbling? How many wonder if they're alone, broken, and unloved? What if someone slowed down to see Vincent Van Gogh—not the painter, but the person? Who knows how much more beauty might have come into the world through this man, by both his brush and his being.

Every day, we have "Van Goghs" in our midst. They may not be world-renowned artists, but they share similar struggles. We pass by people with beauty to create and stories to share, yet many feel unseen. What would happen if we embraced our role as light-bearers among image-bearers, going to the grocery store clerks, the soccer moms, the quiet coworkers, and the overworked dads who stumble? Through intentional radical kindness we can enter into the landscape of the lives of those around us. We have a message of hope that flips on the lights, and shows the path of Christ, "which shines brighter and brighter until full day" (Prov. 4:18). If the world has given up on the light in a church building, then maybe, just maybe, they'll see the Light in us.

• Reflection Questions •

1. Reflect on a person in your life who focused on you. How did that make you feel? Do you remember how they looked at you, sat with you, or stood beside you?

2. What other stories from Scripture show that Jesus saw people?

3. In what ways did Jesus focus on people in that moment?

4. Do you think focus is a superpower? How can you exercise focus more fully?

5. Have you ever had someone in your life try to fix, change, correct, or instruct you, but you didn't believe they valued you? How did that make you feel?

6. Why do you believe we are distracted people? What are we looking for?

7. In what ways do you think screen time increases your loneliness?

8. How do you become distracted in the presence of others? What is one method you can try tomorrow to better focus on someone?

5

RESPOND

In demonstrating what it meant to be a good neighbor, the Samaritan defined the meaning of love. Love doesn't look away. And it doesn't walk away. It involves itself. It inconveniences itself. It indebts itself.[1]
—Ken Gire

A successful attorney once tried to back Jesus into a corner. He sought an answer to one of life's most pressing questions: "What do I need to do to inherit eternal life?" (see Luke 10:25–37). If a greater life exists beyond this world, we'd all like to know the way to get there. The attorney wanted the silver bullet, the all-encompassing pass to a beautiful eternity.

I love the way Jesus answered questions. He masterfully walked people through the outer layers into the heart of a question, always keeping the big picture in mind. In this instance, Jesus appealed to the man's strength—knowledge of the Jewish law. He asked him, "What is written in the law?" The attorney likely thought of the answer like a math quiz. What is the Pythagorean theorem? Easy, $a2 + b2 = c2$. This answer is pretty clear in the law, so I must be headed to heaven. He replied, "Love God with all I am and love my neighbor as myself." Checkmate. Or so he thought.

Jesus told him, "Yes. Do that, and you will live." Imagine Jesus and the attorney just standing there in awkwardness. The wheels in the attorney's head are spinning. Then, he replies, "Who is my neighbor?" As you know, Jesus doesn't give him names or a group of people. Even as the attorney hopes for an easy answer, one that will confirm he has it all together, Jesus tells a story.

We were created to get swept up in stories. Stories are powerful. Just think of Simba and Mufasa. The storming of Omaha Beach in *Saving Private Ryan*. The Avengers versus Thanos. We revere storytellers like Spielberg, Tolkien, Dickens, and Scorsese. Stories speak to our hearts.

In the story Jesus tells, He paints a picture of a bruised man on the side of the road. Robbed, beaten, bruised, and left for dead, the man lay helpless on a dangerous road. That road from Jerusalem to Jericho is a 17-mile route filled with twists, turns, boulders, and caves. Criminals often targeted travelers there, hoping to snatch food, money, and valuables. It's no wonder some called this road "The Way of Blood."

Even if the man limped his way to safety, how would he pay an innkeeper? Where would he find food, bandages, or medicine? Who would take care of him?

Any Jewish expert in the law would have known the repulsive nature of a bloodied and potentially deceased man. Touching a dead body would make a Jewish man unclean, unfit for service and inclusion in the community for at least seven days.

Jesus recounts a priest walking down that dangerous road. As he glimpsed the outline of nearly naked and bloody flesh, I'd like to think his heart wrestled for a moment. He knew the law instructed him to help his brother's ox or donkey that has fallen, even more so your brother himself. But the priest likely couldn't shake another thought—touching this man would make him unclean. Spending seven days away from his duties would be a major inconvenience. Ultimately, he passed the man by, veering to the other side of the road to make sure he remained clean.

Then, along came a Levite. Being a subordinate to the priest, his place on the religious totem pole might have led him to be less committed to purity laws than his supervisor. The Levite had a moment of decision. "Do I slow down and care? Or do I nod, and then pass on?" The Levite also chose to pass.

Finally, the most unlikely of characters enters the story: a Samaritan. There's only one word that appropriately describes the overwhelming emotion of Jews toward Samaritans—hate. This was a burning, unrelenting, vicious hate that lasted for generations.

There's a history to this hate. David was the last king in the Old Testament to do a good job of holding together all of God's people. His son, Solomon, did little to preserve unity, and upon his death the entire network of God's people fractured in two. From then on, a larger northern kingdom, Israel (with Samaria as the capital) and a small southern kingdom, Judah (with Jerusalem as the capital) remained separate. Geographically, the two capitals were only 35 miles apart, but the deep animosity between them made dozens of miles feel like thousands.

The two groups fought about countless things, but the biggest contention was always the appropriate location of worship. Although smaller and less populous, the southern kingdom of Judah housed the great temple built by Solomon. Left to fend for themselves spiritually, the northerners formed their own places of worship, placing golden calf statues at their center.

Amidst this divide, the Assyrians captured the Israelite capital of Samaria around 700 BC. More than 25,000 Jewish peoples were deported to foreign lands. Later, the Babylonians defeated the southern nation and took over Jerusalem. Judeans never forgot which kingdom had fallen first, attributing this failure to the idolatry of golden calves and, even more despicable, the Israelites' intermarriage with Assyrians. Not only were the Jews in Samaria a conquered people; they were now a people with impurity in their bloodline. For generations, Jews in Judah were taught to hate Samaritans.

So Jesus, like a savvy casting director, placed a Samaritan right in the middle of the plot. Jesus knew this would create maximum dissonance in the attorney's mind. If you'd asked the attorney to rank a list of people most likely to inherit eternal life—and the people most likely to exhibit neighborly care—a priest and a Levite would easily crack the top 5. A Samaritan wouldn't even make the list.

But in contrast to the priest and Levite, the Samaritan is moved to compassion by the sight of the bloodied man. The

Greek word used for *compassion* in Luke 10 literally means "to be moved in the guts." It's the same word used to describe the emotion of Jesus when He saw a great crowd of people as though they were sheep without a shepherd. When the Samaritan saw someone hurting, he felt the way Jesus felt. What a tremendous goal for all of us.

The Samaritan helped the broken man to his feet, bandaged him, and poured oil and wine on his wounds. Maybe this was all that the Samaritan had with him. This is what I love about seeing people. We don't have to be experts. We don't have to have deep resources. We don't need to be amazingly articulate or powerfully influential. Don't focus on what you can't do. Do what you can.

At this point, the Samaritan could have said, "There's my good deed for the day." But he didn't. He placed the man on his own animal and walked beside it. He brought him to an inn and took on financial responsibility for his care throughout the night. We can just imagine the broken man opening his eyes the next morning to the sight of a stranger—a Samaritan at that—attending to him. Joel Green describes the act this way: "The care the Samaritan offers is not a model of moral obligation but of exaggerated action grounded in compassion that risks much more than could ever be required or expected."[2]

Is it possible to go overboard with our care, love, and concern for others? The Samaritan gave bandages, oil, wine, lodging, and time to a person that he did not know. Surely, that's enough grace. But is there such a thing as enough grace? Even after all of this, the Samaritan took things a step further, giving two days' wages to the innkeeper, and an additional blank check for continuing care.

After telling this story, Jesus asked the attorney, "Which of these three—priest, Levite, or Samaritan—was the proven neighbor." The attorney replied, "The one who showed him mercy." Jesus's simple reply must has stopped him in his tracks:

"You go, and do likewise." (Luke 10:37)

Jesus wanted this attorney to see people—all people, not just the ones he'd classify as "neighbors." He was reminding this Jewish man not to pick and choose who to value, focus on, or respond to—and He's reminding us too. Seeing people is about value, focus, and response. The Samaritan valued the broken man. He didn't see him as a violation of religious law or a huge inconvenience. He saw a human being, an image-bearer. He focused on him, so much so that he felt it in his guts. He slowed down and drew in. Then, he responded to his needs with overwhelming, over-the-top kindness and intentionality. When we feel like we've delivered too much unexpected grace, too much kindness, and too much generosity—that's probably the moment we're just getting started.

Let's rewind to the attorney's original question. He asked, "Teacher, what shall I do to inherit eternal life?" (v. 25). We allow Scripture to interpret Scripture, and a host of cross references show that good works are not the way to eternal life.

For by grace you have been saved through faith. And this is not your own doing; it is the

gift of God, not a result of works, so that no
one may boast. (Eph. 2:8–9)

We are saved by grace through faith, and Jesus certainly
wasn't confused about this. He wasn't telling the man to do
good works to earn eternal life. Through this story, He was
showing the man what a life ruled by the love and truth of God
looks like. Those who give up their autonomy to make Jesus
king live according to His way. We are called to submit our
lives to the kingship of Jesus, which means He has authority to
define our neighbor.

Ephesians 2:10 goes on to tell us, "For we are his workmanship, created in Christ Jesus for good works, which God
prepared beforehand, that we should walk in them." We are the
workmanship of God, which shows our tremendous value. We
are bespoke, crafted, original works of divine art. Everything
good we do should flow out of the value bestowed on us by
our heavenly Father. God has work for us to do. God always
intended for us to see people. Now, it is our responsibility to
walk in that beautiful purpose. Jesus said, "Give without pay"
and "Go, and do likewise."

The kingdom of Jesus is not stingy with compassion. In
Matthew 5, Jesus goes so far as to tell us to love our enemies.
He explains that everybody loves people who love them back.
But the way of the kingdom is wildly different. If we believe a
certain person doesn't deserve to be counted as our neighbor,
that may be the very person Jesus wants us to see. Eugene
Peterson said, "The Jesus way wedded to the Jesus truth brings
about the Jesus life. We can't proclaim the Jesus truth but then

do it any old way we like. Nor can we follow the Jesus way without speaking the Jesus truth."[3]

Who does Jesus call us to see? In short, anyone—just as He did. Jesus saw fishermen, sick people, paralytics, lepers, children, women, the rich, the poor, the blind, the mute, religious people, irreligious people, spiritually confused people, people who achieved a lot, people who achieved very little, the hungry, the demon-possessed, the doubter, single people, married people, government officials, His friends, His enemies, criminals, rule-followers, rule-breakers, and people from other countries. Jesus saw them all. Don Carson says Jesus is "the ultimate Good Samaritan who comes to broken people condemned to death, and binds up their wounds, and saves their lives and frees them forever from slavery because He pays it all."[4]

One of my mentors served as a pastor for most of his adult life. He was once asked by a younger pastor what kind of people his church was trying to reach. My mentor replied, "People." Not satisfied with the answer, the young pastor pressed, "I know, but what demographic of people? What age or lifestyle of people are you focusing on?" My mentor replied, "People. People are who we are focused on." We should not have a target demographic for our care. People are God's people, and people must be our people. We are called to see people like Jesus saw them.

Don't Hold Back

James, the brother of Jesus, wrote this in James 2:15–17: "If a brother or sister is poorly clothed and lacking in daily food, and one of you says to them, 'Go in peace, be warmed and filled,' without giving them the things needed for the body, what good is that? So also faith by itself, if it does not have works, is dead." Knowledge, study, and understanding are important in our faith. That knowledge should then inspire us toward action. A true knowledge of the magnificence of the Father and the value He holds for His people leads us to live out our faith by exhibiting an astonishing level of care and compassion.

Proverbs 3:27 instructs us, "Do not withhold good from those to whom it is due, when it is in your power to do it." We're called to hold nothing back. We can't treat good as though it's an irreplaceable commodity. We often have a tendency to disobey or disregard commands from God, but all of His instructions exist for a reason. Why would God have to tell us not to withhold good? Because we have a tendency to withhold good. This verse prompts us to examine the deeper reasons we hold back good from others. Do we think that if we give it away, we won't have enough of it for ourselves? Do we believe that doing good will exhaust us? Galatians 6:9 tells us, "And let us not grow weary of doing good, for in due season we will reap, if we do not give up."

It scares us to think of giving ourselves away. When we slow down, focus, and respond to others, it sometimes feels like tearing a little piece of ourselves off and handing it to another person. If we keep up that practice, we may imagine becoming a mental and emotional zombie, dragging a leg and grunting at everyone who passes by. People can be exhausting, right?

Instead, we should look at our lives like a bucket, so filled with the love of our heavenly Father and the grace that Christ offers that we overflow into the world around us. Ephesians 1:8 shows us that our Father *lavished* on us the riches of the grace shown to us in the good news of Jesus. The English word *lavish* means "sumptuously rich, elaborate, or luxurious."[5] The riches of the grace of Christ to us are luxurious. The Greek word for lavish means to exceed the ordinary, to overflow, or to be over and above. The grace of Christ is so abundant that we have barns of it out back full and ready for our present and future sin. God has not been stingy with His grace, and neither should we be. For every ounce we pour out on others, we'll be filled to the brim again by God.

How do we stay spiritually full? Seeing others requires us to continually refresh our hearts and minds in the presence of our heavenly Father. In our emptiness, we draw near to Him who renews and reminds us of His grace and love. The gospel work of Christ opens the door to the office of God so that we may walk in, sit down, and chat with our Father. First John 5:14–15 tells us, "And this is the confidence that we have toward him, that if we ask anything according to his will he hears us. And if we know that he hears us in whatever we ask, we know that we have the requests that we have asked of him."

Prayer—and practicing the presence of God in prayer—fuels our ability to see others.

When the prophet Jeremiah fell to a point of despair, even thinking that the Lord has forgotten him, He cried out to God, "But this I call to mind, and therefore I have hope: The steadfast love of the LORD never ceases; his mercies never come to an end; they are new every morning; great is your faithfulness" (Lam. 3:21–23).

Kara Tippetts, a pastor's wife and mother of four in Colorado Springs, died at the age of thirty-eight, just two years after learning she had stage four breast cancer. Kara inspired hundreds of thousands of people with her perspective on love, pain, and the grace of Jesus, even while she was suffering. A documentary on her life was released in 2019 with the title, *The Long Goodbye: The Kara Tippetts Story.* In her final months, Kara asked the simple question, "Why is it that we withhold love? Why?"[6] Sometimes the question is not, "What is most profitable?" or "What is most fun?" Rather, the question is "How can I best love others?"

Flying VFR

If we want to see people the way Jesus saw people, we must value people, focus on people, and respond to the real needs of people. The words *value, focus*, and *respond* form the acrostic V-F-R. But that abbreviation also means something else. When the pilot of an airplane flies VFR, they are flying by Visual Flight Rules. Flying VFR can only happen in favorable weather, since it involves constantly watching over the nose of the airplane and around the wings for landmarks, weather condition changes, and other aircraft. Flying by IFR, or Instrument Flight Rules, involves using the instrumentation of the aircraft to follow a specific, predetermined path of flight.

A friend of mine is a flight instructor, and he once invited me along on a student flight where his student was learning to fly IFR. I love flying on commercial aircraft, so I jumped at the opportunity to ride along. Shortly after takeoff, I realized a few things quickly:

1. Small aircraft flight is very bumpy.
2. The back seat of a small aircraft is uncomfortable and smells a little weird.
3. The term *student pilot* should carry the same danger-inducing fear as the term *student brain surgeon* or *student skydiving instructor.*

My friend was a fantastic instructor, which was a good thing, because this young pilot needed a lot of instruction. While learning to fly IFR, the student pilot wore glasses that shielded his vision from everything except the instruments below the front window. Hearing my groans from the backseat, the pilot would turn around with those odd glasses and ask me if I was okay. With the glasses on, I believe he could only see me from my knees down. I was technically fine, if a little queasy, but I was desperately wishing he'd take off those glasses and figure out how to fly in a straight line.

We often fly through our days on IFR. We follow the specific, predetermined path of our own agenda. We have coffee meetings, soccer practice drop-offs, concerts, client meetings, lesson plans, and family functions. We're tempted to speed through errands and even speed past people. When our eyes remain fixed exclusively on the tasks ahead, we miss countless chances to value people, focus, and respond to the opportunities that Jesus brings into our field of vision. Grocery trips can become prayer walks when we're aware that the people picking out bananas and waiting for their deli order are image-bearers of God. Instead of scrolling through social media in our air-conditioned vehicles while soccer practice wraps up, we can take a few moments to connect with a fellow parent. All those front doors around you represent homes full of valuable people who are waiting for a neighbor to truly see them.

5 Practical Ways to Respond

Seeing people takes not just our eyes, but also our time, energy, and effort. Here are five practical ways that we can see others by responding to them.

1. Words

You've been the recipient of a good word. A teacher, father, mother, friend, pastor, or neighbor once said the right thing at the right time, and you'll never forget it. Proverbs 12:25 says, "Anxiety in a man's heart weighs him down, but a good word makes him glad." The mental effects of the COVID-19 pandemic appear to have increased the level of perceived anxiety. In January 2019, a U.S. Census Bureau survey reported that 11 percent of the respondents indicated symptoms of anxiety or depression. By the following December 2020, the percentage nearly quadrupled to more than 42 percent.[7] Clinical psychologist Luana Marques from Harvard Medical School concluded, "I don't think this is going to go back to baseline anytime soon."[8] As beneficiaries of the grace of Jesus, we have the opportunity to shoot arrows of hope into the multiplying anxiety in the world.

Amidst delegation and direction, we should share affirming words with employees and students. Our children and friends need to hear us point out acts of good character and achievement. Something as simple as "I noticed your hard work today, thank you" can be the right words to uplift the weary. We've all wondered if someone were watching, and whether we were making a difference. Our affirmation should be sincere, specific, and based on actual strengths of the recipient.

Also, we should learn to demonstrate empathy with our words. A recent study by the American Psychological Association revealed that humans have "mirror neurons." Researchers concluded that watching an action and performing an action can also elicit the same feelings in people. Neuroscientist Vittorio Gallese says, "It seems we're wired to see other people as similar to us, rather than different. . . . At the root, as humans we identify the person we're facing as someone like ourselves."[9] We are wired, or created by God, to empathize with others. Therefore, we should develop our gift of empathy as a well-trained skill.

Sympathy happens when we think, *I can imagine me feeling what you feel.* But empathy goes one step further. In empathy, we think, *I can imagine you feeling what you feel.* In empathy, we are not viewing others through the lens of ourselves. We can draw in and listen intently without filtering a person's words through our own experience. Exercising empathy doesn't imply that we agree with the entirety of a person's actions. We don't have to understand everything about a situation before we act in empathy. Listening, intently and without pretense, sets the stage for love and care.

A classroom setting is a great opportunity to see people through the words we share. Teachers are game-changers and heroes. But teaching can be a grind. It can be easy to start seeing not individual students but a sea of children or teenagers in a room. Yet what if we drew into the grace we receive from our heavenly Father, to then overflow into individual students in the room? Students are more than their behavior or their efforts to elude us with their glances at a phone. They're image-bearers of God before they are anything else. At the beginning of each school day, what if you wrote down the name of one student that day to go over and above with in your affirmation, listening, and care? Rotate through all of your students. With twenty-five students in a classroom, and about 175 days in a school year, a teacher could have seven unique opportunities with each student to show them not just a lesson plan or correction, but the seeing eyes, listening ears, and words from a teacher who loves them for who God made them to be.

Have you ever had someone wrong you? It's heartbreaking how sometimes the closest of friends and family members can become enemies. As a pastor, I've received some heartbreaking words from the people I've been called to care for. One thought from a close pastor friend has moved me to deal with challenging people with grace. He said, "Imagine that the person who wronged you is someone else's son or daughter. If your own son or daughter messed up, you'd want people to treat them with truth *and* gentleness." As gospel people, we are sons and daughters of our heavenly Father, and we have wronged Him in our sin and rebellion. But He deals with us with truth and grace. He doesn't dunk on us but made a way for forgiveness by pouring out wrath on His own Son. The gospel moves us to do the same with others.

In John 20:21, Jesus says to His followers, "Peace be with you. As the Father has sent me, even so I am sending you." As sent ones, we don't merely have client lists, patients, students, children, coworkers, customers, and team members. Seth Godin said, "We don't change markets, or populations, we change people. One person at a time, at a human level. And often, that change comes from small acts that move us, not from grand pronouncements."[10] Do you know your clients? Not just their needs as a customer, but do you know *them*? Have you asked, "What is difficult in your life right now?" This can seem like a pastor-type question, and you may not see yourself as a pastor. But as followers of Jesus, we are a sent people, and our mission is the world in front of us and all around us.

Author and entrepreneur Roche Mamabolo shares that "caring has become a huge competitive advantage."[11] He goes on to say that the secret to disruptive innovation and technology is not just about disrupting an industry. Roche explains that the secret is disrupting the lives of ordinary people for the better. Let's be grace-filled, gospel-driven disrupters in a world that God loves and Christ died for.

2. Gifts

The next time you visit a restaurant, take time to learn the person's name who takes your order, refills your drink, and brings your food. Ask them questions about their life. Are they wearing a bracelet to remember a friend or family member? Did they share a detail of their life with you? Remember that. Listen. Draw in. Use the person's name at the end of the meal and thank them for creating a beautiful experience for you to enjoy your food and time with others. After the meal, take it a step further. Based on what you heard in your conversation, how could you follow up? What if you brought them an appropriately worded handwritten note with a small gift card to a coffee shop? I waited tables in college for nearly four years, and I can't recall one person who followed up after the meal with such intentionality.

The key to being a great gift-giver is to be a good listener. We don't have to spend a lot of money to give a gift that is intentional. When you think of giving a good gift, think of the acrostic P-S-T. When you whisper to someone in a quiet situation, you might say, "Pssst." You are interrupting their space in a situation where they aren't used to being interrupted. When we see a person by giving the right gift, we are stepping into their space.

- **P** stands for presentation. We don't just flop a box from Amazon down in front of them. Wrap it up, write a small note, attach a thoughtful picture, or think up a rhyme to go along with the gift.
- S stands for surprise. Don't tell them what you're doing or what you're giving. Make it a surprise.
- T stands for thoughtfulness. What did you hear in conversation that could be represented in your choice of a gift?

When you are listening in your group of friends, checking out at the grocery store, or visiting the salon, listen with the intention of action generously. Imagine your stylist sharing with you how much she loves fall weather. She says that it's her favorite season. Follow up with a visit the next day she is working (even when you don't have an appointment) with a gift bag of cider, spices, a candle, or a gift card to a local pumpkin patch. Write a little note to go with it. Compliment her on the good work she did on your hair and tell how much you appreciate her.

Student, vehicle, and credit card debt often make generosity seem out of reach. The average amount of American consumer debt sits at \$34,055. Nearly three out of four Americans (72%) say they are burdened by debt.[12] A part of your journey in seeing people could be getting out of debt and building your ability to exercise generosity. Keep in mind, though, that gifts don't have to be expensive to be intentional and thoughtful.

The good Samaritan didn't just give bandages, oil, and wine. He gave two days' wages and a blank check for future expenses. Maybe you can't give a blank check. What you can do is think P-S-T, and write a note to go along with a gift. Think to yourself, *What is the "innkeeper moment" with this person? What can I do that seems over the top and entirely unexpected?*

3. Presence

Seeing people by showing up is one of my favorite ways to respond to others. Showing up often surprises the person we visit, doesn't cost money (other than gas or subway fare), and is a clear demonstration of a sacrifice or investment of our time in a busy culture. To some, writing a check or buying a gift seems too easy. Gifts don't speak the same way to every person. My wife, for example, is not a gift person. She is more of a saver than a spender, and she also grew up in a family that placed a high value on quality time together. Quality time can be difficult. It can't happen in an instant. You can't buy it. Quality time is also easily broken down by distractions.

We're all busy, and you may think, *Wow, I barely have enough time to get to MY things!* This makes showing up that much more powerful. Time is a precious commodity, and in a hurried and anxious culture, our gift of presence in the life of another is like gold. Here are a few examples of showing up:

- Attend a sporting or arts event of a friend's child.
- Drop by, if it's appropriate, the workplace of a friend—just because. You don't have to stay long, just pop in to say hello.
- Drop by a friend's house, but don't go in. Leave your car running. Tell them, "I was just right by your house and wanted to at least see you for a minute." Have a friend who is just having a tough day or season? Show up, and also bring a small bag of some of their favorite things.
- Book a flight or drive to surprise a person at a big event—a 50th wedding anniversary, retirement party, graduation, or a big birthday milestone. If you fly in just to see a friend, I call this a "$300 hug." It's worth it.
- Find out the name of the hospital and the time of a person's surgery. Ask them, "What time do you have to be at the hospital or surgery center?" Show up at the waiting room (in accordance with hospital visitor rules) to see them and pray for them before their surgery. You'll likely also get to meet family members and display "loving one

another" in front of them. If hospital rules don't allow you to enter the hospital, drive to the hospital parking lot and pray. Snap a pic of the hospital as you're there and send it to them to let them know you're present and you're praying.

- Join in with a person's interests or hobbies. People love pickleball, antiquing, hiking, bird-watching, CrossFit, off-roading, attending sporting events, and the list goes on. Ask them to bring you along or teach you, even if it's just once or twice.

4. Sharing the Gospel

Some people reading this book may wonder why it's taken over four chapters to get to the point of sharing the gospel. I've intentionally waited to share this point. There are already several necessary and great books dedicated to the topic of evangelism. I love evangelism. Evangelism isn't optional or a suggestion. We're all called to take a role in leading those far from God into a saving relationship with Jesus. We are called to good deeds and to speak the good news of the gospel.

Here is where I see this message of seeing people making a *huge* difference in evangelism. When we see people well, we better aim the gospel of Christ in our words. Seeing people well is like an archer who takes time to pull the arrow all the way back. Careful time is given to ensure proper aim, form, and release of the arrow. When we take time to value, focus, and respond, we aim the arrow of the gospel through the depth of our relationship and our personal example of a life following Christ. We don't always have to wait for a deep relationship to share the gospel. I would argue that love sure does help.

What if someone asked you right now, "How can I become a Christian?" Do you have a concise, understandable, and actionable answer to give? You'd be surprised how difficult it is for most Christians to answer this question. Some say that it's trivial to share such a powerful and profound message like the gospel in just a few moments. However, we see in the Scriptures several examples of concise, understandable, and actionable gospel presentations. Peter preached a simple sermon at Pentecost and 3,000 people gave their lives to Christ. Stephen preached the gospel succinctly but brilliantly in Acts 7. Paul preached to King Agrippa in Acts 26.

Let's combine three points for maximum evangelistic effectiveness:

1. Our affections are drawn to the person of Jesus so much so that His love overflows out of our lives. And then . . .
2. We value people, focus on their lives, and respond to their real needs. So then we . . .
3. Clearly communicate the gospel in a way that is concise, understandable, and actionable. What a powerful trio!

5. Prayer

We display our role in the kingdom of Christ when we see our neighbor the way Jesus sees our neighbor. And the way we communicate with our King and Father is through prayer. There may be no greater way that we can see people than to offer genuine, heartfelt, earnest prayers to our Father on behalf of another person. Sometimes people ask for prayer—in a small group, one-on-one, or even on social media. Other times, when we value people and focus on them, we can be prompted to pray as a response to what we see. I'd like to offer three points to keep in mind when we are led to pray on behalf of others.

First, **remember the prayer request**. Has anyone ever asked you to pray, and then an hour later you find it difficult to remember exactly what you're supposed to be praying for? Or have you ever shared a prayer request with another person, and you don't notice them writing it down. Make a habit to remember prayer requests by immediately writing them down in a notebook or on a note on your phone. You'll not only remember the actual prayer request, but you are also communicating to the person that their request is important to you.

I keep my prayer notes in the notes app on my phone, and I remind the person requesting that I'm pulling out my phone to type down the request. I don't want them to think I'm taking focus off them to check a text message or scroll through email. You can also offer a response like, "I don't know what to say right now, but I'm so glad you told me. I will pray for you." You don't have to feel pressure to make the situation better by saying "the right thing." Your presence, intentionality, and earnestness are the best way to communicate care.

Second, make sure to **be consistent** in your prayers for that person. Commit to prayer for a specific time, or until the request is answered. Make prayer for others a consistent part of your time with Jesus. Another way to see people through prayer is to pray in the moment that you hear a prayer request or sense an opportunity to pray. I've prayed for people right in the middle of grocery stores, at baseball stadiums, in parking lots, during Facebook marketplace deals, backyards, and in church buildings. Simply ask, "Can I pray for you right now?" I've never had a person turn me down.

Third, **remind the person** that you are praying for them. Knowing that another person has continued to pray is tremendously encouraging. Send a text message or swing by a person's office and remind them that you are praying, and ask for updates. In a busy, distracted, and often forgetful world, we communicate astonishing care when people know that we are praying for them. For certain requests, I'll create a reminder on my phone that prompts me to pray and check-in with the person.

Our God Is Not Hiding

Psalm 115:3 proclaims, "Our God is in the heavens; he does all that he pleases." I can't control how God works. I can't control if a person will become a follower of Jesus. But I can control my kindness. I can make the conscious decision to live in VFR mode with an anxious culture of people looking for hope in places that won't deliver. Some even believe that God has given up on them, and they've given up on God and religion. Philosopher Bertrand Russell, a well-known atheist, was once asked what he would ask God, given the opportunity. He said he would ask, "Sir, why did you take such pains to hide yourself?" My concern is not that God has chosen to hide Himself. My concern is that too many of His followers are ashamed or unwilling to make Him known.

God has not hidden Himself. In Proverbs 8:17, God offers this promise: "Those who seek me diligently find me." God is findable. The gospel is the good news of the saving work of Jesus. And we, as His followers, are His plan to be His hands and feet on earth. Isaiah 52:7 boldly declares, "How beautiful upon the mountains are the feet of him who brings good news, who publishes peace, who brings good news of happiness, who publishes salvation, who says to Zion, 'Your God reigns.'" Our kindness, gentleness, and intentionality become the bridge by which He may drive His gospel into the hearts of others.

Ray Ortlund, the founding pastor of Immanuel Church in Nashville, Tennessee, often begins services with a welcome that beautifully displays the heart of Jesus. The welcome is an adaptation from James Boice of Tenth Presbyterian Church. Being reminded of the attitude of Jesus gives us a point to orient our own hearts around. Ortlund, with his gentle and warm voice, addresses his congregation with this:

> To all who are weary and need rest;
> To all who mourn and long for comfort;

To all who feel worthless and wonder if God
    even cares;
To all who are weak and fail and desire
    strength;
To all who sin and need a Savior—
This church opens wide her doors with a wel-
    come from Jesus,
the mighty friend of sinners.[13]

May we share that same heart, as Christ has also welcomed us.

• Reflection Questions •

1. Take a moment to think of a person who is difficult for you to see. Why is it hard for you to see them? You don't have to use their name in discussion.

2. What are some ways that others have made you feel seen? What did they do for you? How did that make you feel?

3. Have you ever witnessed or participated in an "innkeeper moment," where someone was lavished with kindness and generosity? What was that like?

4. Who do you need to see today? How can you see them by responding to them?

6

COLLECTIVE SIGHT

*If you want to go fast, go alone. If you
want to go far, go together.*[1]
—African Proverb

Chris is tall, smiles a lot, and I've even heard people say that he has an "orbit." If you get within a few feet of him, you can feel his positive energy and enthusiasm. There aren't many people like him. As a business owner, husband, and father of four, he spins a lot of plates. But when you're with him, he always offers his undivided attention. Frederick Buechner defines vocation as the place where "your deep gladness and the world's deep hunger meet."[2] For Chris, work is more than an occupation or a way to create an income. His business, and the people who make it go, are a calling.

When Chris and I were classmates in seminary, he turned toward me one day with his enormous smile and boundless energy and asked if I would design a logo for his new business. He said he wanted it to look "fast." There aren't many seminary students looking to launch a business symbolized by speed, but like I said, there aren't many people like Chris. I obliged, and created a red, white, and blue logo for his one-man company.

Today, Chris is known as the founder and CEO of Booster. He first had the idea for the Booster Fun Run when he was a college student at Samford University. Forty-nine school principals told him he had a good idea but they'd rather wait until another school tried it first. Then, one said yes. The school needed to raise $3,000. Chris, with his ambition to serve his clients well and create an amazing experience for students, raised the school an astounding $22,000. The school was beyond thrilled, of course, and Booster took off—despite that hideous first logo by yours truly.

Under Chris's leadership and client-focused care, at the time of this writing Booster has served 7,500 school partners raising over $600,000,000 to improve education. Chris sits on multiple school advisory boards, has won Atlanta's prestigious 40 Under 40 Award, and even earned the President's Council on Sports, Fitness, & Nutrition Community Award in 2016, an honor bestowed by the White House to leaders across the country who promote fitness in their local communities. Chris has a passion to create a remarkable company culture—one that cares for coworkers and clients, attracts and develops great leaders, and celebrates people like no other company I've ever seen. And every year, Chris calls his first-ever client to say "thank you" for taking a chance on a twenty-two-year-old with a big idea.

Booster has raised hundreds of millions of dollars for local schools, but they have done so without sacrificing a culture of care and value for employees and clients alike. I interviewed Chris for this book at a two-day gathering of his general managers from around the country. I arrived early to the venue and he invited me to sit in on one of the sessions, a workshop led by a mental health counselor teaching leaders how best to care for the mental health needs of their employees. This is what Chris does. By investing in his managers, he invests in the lives of everyone in his organization. Each employee is not merely a cog in a wheel. Each is a person who will climb every mountain you attempt to summit—when you believe in them and see them.

Self-admittedly, Chris is an impatient person and has to force himself to take the long view. He said, "If you plant seeds, you won't have apples tomorrow morning." Seeing employees and clients may not immediately impact profit, but exercising patience and care will impact employee satisfaction and well-being, which can lead to greater productivity and retention.[3] Booster has developed a culture of care. They celebrate not only business accomplishments, but personal life events within their company.

I asked Chris how he has created an organization that profits steadily while continuing to see people with such intentionality. His answer was simple: "People." Culture starts with people. Booster promotes individuals in the company who have demonstrated that they can contribute to the direct profits of the organization while demonstrating compassion, care, and celebration for fellow employees and clients. You create great culture with great people.

Because Booster employees are provided with a sense of value and significance, the organization was able to retain every general manager and every leadership team member through the COVID-19 pandemic. During this difficult season, the organization embraced three key values: transparency, trust, and togetherness. They ran their cash reserves down to challenging lows. But even when Chris's employees received job offers with higher salaries and more immediate security, they stayed because of the culture of care, enthusiasm, and significance they get working on the Booster team.

Collective Sight in the Early Church

The preceding chapters focused on individuals seeing each other, mostly in one-on-one interactions. I want to talk in this chapter about something called collective sight. Exhibiting collective sight is not a new concept. The early church came together to see those in need. They learned sound doctrine, broke bread together, and prayed. But their faith wasn't mere head knowledge. They did something, and they did it together.

In Acts 6, we see tremendous numerical growth of the church. It was growing so fast that a group within the church, the Hellenist widows, were neglected in care. The apostles didn't create a false dichotomy between care and doctrine, leaving behind teaching in order to meet the physical needs of the people. Instead, they continued to share the gospel and pray, instructing the church to choose from among themselves a group of mature believers who could dedicate themselves to the physical care of this neglected group. The church now had a leadership structure committed to doctrinal integrity, prayer, community and caring for physical needs. With a new vision for all-encompassing mission and care, the church "multiplied greatly" (Acts 6:7).

One example of collective sight is described in Acts 2. The church listened to sound teaching, ate meals together, and prayed. They gathered for worship and thanked the Lord for all they had. But they weren't just blessing-collectors. They were over-the-top, crazy generous with what they were given. Acts 2:44 says that they held all things in common. Some have mistakenly equated this to a form of socialism. When we look closer, we see the way of the kingdom of Jesus is peculiar. It's odd and foreign to our earthly constructed views of earning and consumption. His ways are higher and greater than any system formed by man.

The early church held such a passion for care that they collectively worked to serve those in need. They saw intentionality and responsibility as a team sport. Their personal compensation was not merely for their personal consumption—they chose to give it away. When they didn't have enough to meet the needs of others, they sold belongings and distributed the proceeds to any who had need (Acts 2:45). The needs were often large enough to require several individuals and families to pool their resources.

Partly because of this radical care and generosity, Christianity spread like wildfire in the first few centuries after Jesus's death and resurrection. Government leaders began to question the motives and practices of those who converted from Judaism and even paganism to this new way. Around

AD 125, a Christian philosopher named Aristedes looked at Christians in his day and concluded:

> They walk in all humility and kindness, and falsehood is not found among them, and they love one another. They despise not the widow, and grieve not the orphan. . . . And if there is a man among them that is poor and needy, and they have not among them an abundance of necessaries, they fast two or three days that they may supply the needy with their necessary food.[4]

Have you ever heard someone say, "I'm not that into organized religion"? If organized religion means judgmental people and stale rituals, then I'm not into organized religion either. But if organized religion means collaborating together to see others and providing the kind of care that none of us could offer individually, then I'm all in. Perhaps if others saw us offering that kind of love and generosity, they'd be into organized religion too.

Let's See People, Together

Collective sight isn't just for nonprofit organizations. What would it look like for your business, school, family, or neighborhood to see people collectively? In our home, the question "Who did you see today?" has changed the tone and nature of the dinner table discussions. Whenever we ask, "What did you do at school today?" We usually get either "Nothing" or "Went to classes, recess, same stuff." But the question "Who did you see today?" is different. It prompts our kids to think about the actual people they encountered. Knowing they'll be asked this question also encourages them to have an answer to the question the next day. If they know their mom and dad will listen to their responses and cheer them on, they'll have their eyes up—off of their devices and onto the students around them. Young people need to be seen, and other young people can be the change-makers who show them that they're valuable.

Collective sight happens when two or more individuals come together in order to see people together better than they could do individually. The formula looks like this:

(Value + Focus + Response) | Multiplied |
By a Collection of People

A person seeing another person is awesome. More than one individual coming together to see a person is even more powerful. "You thought of me!" is good. "You all thought of me!" is even better.

What if you began staff meetings with stories of people in your organization who see other people well? Throw out that question, "Who did you see today?" If they know you, as the leader, are going to ask, then they'll be more likely to think of seeing others during the workday and even at home. Leaders demonstrate values by the questions we ask, and asking these questions costs us nothing and offers an incredible reward in our team culture.

One study showed that 63 percent of millennials believe the primary purpose of businesses should be "improving society" instead of "generating profit." If you communicate, whether implicitly or explicitly, that profit is the most important variable, you'll miss the opportunity to engage the hearts of millennial employees.[5] Jesus said it this way: "For what will it profit a man if he gains the whole world and forfeits his soul? Or what shall a man give in return for his soul?" (Matt. 16:26).

What kind of a difference would it make in your homeowners' association to discuss more than mulch around the playground or the operating hours of the community pool. Instead, ask, "How can we care for those in and around our community?" Something interesting happens when we serve shoulder to shoulder alongside others. We find out it's difficult to be angry and fight with one another when we are serving together. By nature, when we reduce our goals to a single variable (profit, homeowner satisfaction, wins, grades, rules, etc.), we lose total sight of everything else we could be doing that's often more important than that one variable.

A slightly different question that's well worth asking: "How do you need to be seen today?" In doing this, you can explain that we all need to be seen. Life is often challenging, and we need grace, both from God and others. This question demonstrates that you care for people as people, not just as a source of productivity. Employees are looking for care that goes far beyond a birthday cake and a picture on a bulletin board. We often ask this question in our Sunday night family meeting.

Our kiddos will respond, "I have a huge test this week, and I might be a little on edge." Another child has responded, "I'm nervous about my upcoming cross-country meet." I once told my family, "I have a lot of important appointments coming up, and I want to do a better job of trusting Jesus in the pressure of church life." We all need to be seen, but it's being humble enough to admit it that makes a difference. We need to see people before they have to ask to be seen.

What do we get when we join together in collective sight? Togetherness, community, and unity. The English-language word "community" derives from an older French word that simply means "public spirit." How might the public spirit of our organizations change when each member understands that their work contributes to the impact of real people in the world? It's more difficult to be angry or divisive toward supervisors and coworkers when you're working together for the common good of something greater than your organization.

There's a reason why members of football teams are often closer to one another than members of a book club. Members of a football team have a job to do. They train together, hurt together, and celebrate together. There's nothing wrong with book clubs, but members of a book club don't usually have a long-term common goal. There is no scoreboard in a book club. Each member of the team needs to understand the "why" behind what they do. Collectively, when we choose to celebrate our united impact, it's more difficult to remain angry or dissatisfied. It's hard to point fingers and play armchair quarterback when we work shoulder-to-shoulder.

What do you all do here?

Taking your chances on a new barber is inherently risky, but sometimes I like to live life on the edge. While my regular barber was on vacation, I had the opportunity to see a new person on staff. We'll call her "Sarah." Sarah had a pleasant and calm spirit, and she welcomed me as I sat down in her chair. We exchanged a few pleasantries before she asked me the big question: "What do you do for a living?" I've been a pastor long enough to know that this is a make-or-break question. Some people get more comfortable in conversation with me; other times, things get awkward fast. I told her that I was a pastor, and she responded with both a smile and a slight tear in her eye. She was silent for what seemed like five minutes and then asked, "As a pastor, do you do counseling? My husband and I need help." I said, "Of course; when would y'all like to sit down and talk?"

I learned later in that initial conversation with Sarah that they were Jewish, and they didn't have a close relationship with their rabbi. Sarah and I set up a time for the three of us to meet at my office. I felt for her husband, imagining Sarah coming home from work and saying, "Honey, I had a pastor in my chair today, and you've never met him, but I'd like for us to sit down with him and share our struggles." Not an easy conversation. He could have said, "No way," but he didn't.

I met Sarah's husband on a cool fall evening outside the doors of my office. He was a big guy, a beard, and a firm handshake. His demeanor was about what you would imagine a husband's demeanor to be if your wife brought you along to a conversation with a Protestant church pastor who you'd never meet. I sensed aloofness, nervousness, and desperation all mixed into one. I'll never forget the first question that he asked me. It's a question that I've passed along to our church staff and church family on a number of occasions. I've shared the question with pastor friends and church leaders. Every time I share it, people respond, "Wow, that's a great question."

Sarah's husband said to me, "I've never been to a church before, but I've always wondered when I drive by—What do you all do here?" I wish I'd had a month to think up a perfect answer. Hurriedly, I responded, "We help people know and follow Jesus." Then, we went on in conversation to unpack their present circumstances and a potential path forward. I listened, offered the hope of Jesus in the gospel, and prayed with them.

Every company, family, school, and business could also explore the answer to that question. "What do you all do here?" Increase profits, build gadgets, deliver a worthwhile service, teach curriculum, efficiently handle the schedule—absolutely. But what do we do here for individual people? How do we make an impact? How do you add to the collective good in your community?

The Center for Creative Leadership (CCL) published an article detailing the importance of creating a sense of meaning and significance in the employee work environment. Specifically, CCL put forth two tangible ways to boost employee buy-in and retention. First, organizations and companies should share tangible positive outcomes and real impact of care initiatives. Be specific about dollars given away, recyclable materials used, or scholarships granted. Second, make sure you don't make "much ado about nothing." I once heard William Vanderbloemen say, "Fun and healthy culture are not the same thing."[6] Creating a healthy culture doesn't necessarily begin with fun. It begins with creating a sense of significance in work.

Be authentic and specific in your description of care initiatives. Disingenuously communicating care will do much damage. CCL's study concluded, "Almost 85% of Millennials believe making a positive difference in the world is more important than professional recognition." The respondents also remarked, "If my organization is helping to save the world, I am too. I feel good about the work I do."[7]

Practical ways to exhibit collective sight

How can your organization exhibit greater collective sight? Here are four ideas to make collective sight a part of your family, company, or organization.

Make it personal. The more personal we can make our standard and practice of care, the more effective our care will be. Caring for the poor is a worthy endeavor. We could simply choose an organization, write checks, and celebrate numbers. However, what if we instead connected to an organization that appropriately showed the stories of those facing homelessness or food insecurity. Instead of thinking of "the poor," we could imagine an unemployed or underemployed single mother named Lisa working to provide for her two children. Employees could be educated on the reasons and demographics of those facing poverty. The more we connect to individual stories instead of vague demographics, the greater the impact our care efforts will have.

Our church in the Atlanta area wants to do everything we can to positively impact the foster care system in Georgia. Currently, there are more than 14,000 children in care in our state. We talk about the foster system often because we believe it is the responsibility of every Christ-follower to consider how we can care for vulnerable children. We try to make it personal by having real foster families tell their foster journey stories—the good, the bad, and the ugly.

One of my favorite stories in the life of our church involves a married couple who had been fostering two wonderful little girls. The couple came from a very ritualistic, formal, and rules-oriented branch of religion. The husband and wife brought their girls to their former place of worship, but the local church leaders had no idea how to serve their family well. The couple began to ask around about churches that expressed and demonstrated an openness to families with children in the foster system. Another foster family told them, "If you have foster kids, Northside Church is the place to gather and grow." I don't know if I've ever heard a better compliment to the people of our church.

Imagine the impact on our kids' ministry workers when this foster mother stood on a stage and told the story of their family being welcomed to the church. She talked about how our workers got down on one knee, looked into the eyes of their little girls, remembered their names, and integrated them into the life of the kids' ministry. There was not a dry eye in the room. Their story made it personal for our ministry team.

Make it fun. Collective sight doesn't have to be a solemn affair. Achieving a common goal can (and should) be exciting. The situations we are called to step into are often bittersweet. Our demonstration of love and enthusiasm can be the difference-maker for those we collectively see and serve. In Greek, the word *enthusiasm* literally means "God in me." We should demonstrate enthusiasm and strive to lead organizations that demonstrate the hope of the Lord is in us.

In my early years of student ministry, a high school student developed a passion to build a house for a family in Haiti. After a brainstorming session about funding, we came up with the idea to build a clear, acrylic house, 30 inches square by 30 inches tall—a piggy bank of sorts that could hold pennies students donated toward the effort of building the house. We made it fun, and students got on board. They wiped out almost every bank in the area with thousands and thousands of pennies. I walked into one local bank and the teller immediately told me, "Please, don't ask for any more pennies. We are completely out."

We had done the math on the cubic inches of pennies necessary to come up with the $3,000 to build a house in Haiti. The math we had not done was how much all those pennies would weigh. With the house just half full, it weighed over 800 pounds and was impossible to move. The penny-filled house eventually broke a countertop on which it was sitting, spilling tens of thousands of pennies all over the ground. We had a local carpenter build what we called a "Mega Stand" and were able to collect more than 300,000 pennies which weighed more than 1,600 pounds. That project was so fun, and now a family in Haiti has a house built by the generosity of middle and high school students.

Celebrate it. You grow what you celebrate. If you have a mission statement on paper or on the wall, and you don't celebrate the results of the mission, your mission is nothing more than a collection of words. We often do a good job of getting in a room and brainstorming the specific purpose of what we do. But when it comes to everyday work, we often forget to stop and celebrate the fruit. Maybe you already have initiatives in your organization aimed at caring for those outside the organization. Have you celebrated those initiatives? In your staff meetings, company parties, and newsletters, do you consistently talk about the impact that your employees are making?

Start with one employee or a group of employees in your organization who embody what it means to see people. Call them out. Chris from Booster shared with me that their organization often slows down to take the opportunity to call out the good in one another. At a local gathering of their regional leaders, Chris asked each person to encourage others by answering the question, "What is something redemptive and encouraging you have seen in someone else's life?" In a beautiful outdoor setting with large tables, candles, and lights, members of his team celebrated the good works that they saw from others. It wasn't about profits. It was about people.

Put someone in charge. Someone in your organization needs to be the "Chief Care Officer." Your company or organization could add as a part of your C-suite a formal position charged with vetting and championing what collective sight will look like. They should be the go-to for enthusiasm, effectively communicating how you will impact the world beyond profits and scores. Collective work requires people, and people need care. The bigger the organization, the more care your organization will need. If you're not able to create a formal position, maybe one person would love to be responsible for helping the company work together for the good of the community. Someone has to be the champion. We have leaders for everything we deem to be most important—facilities, accounting, human resources, research and development, and leadership. Why not place someone in charge of collective sight?

What do you want your organization to be known for? Producing great products? Excellent services? Certainly. But what if your organization were known for more? If your organization no longer existed, would the local community lament the loss? A dream without a goal is just a wish. And a wish, without someone in charge, isn't going anywhere. People lose loved ones, struggle with loneliness, parenting, and mental and physical health. Members of your team will work better and you'll have higher retention if your people truly believe that you care for them—for not just what they do but for who they are. Demonstrate value for others such that you invest in the necessary people and positions to provide care for the people who make your organization go.

Start Where You Are

Arthur Ashe broke the norms of professional tennis when he became the first black player selected to the United States Davis Cup team and the only black man ever to win the singles title at Wimbledon, the US Open, and the Australian Open. Known for his philanthropic efforts off the court, he founded the Arthur Ashe Foundation for the Defeat of AIDS and the Arthur Ashe Institute for Urban Health. He was posthumously awarded the Presidential Medal of Freedom in 1993. Ashe brought individuals together to see people collectively. Despite his achievements, Ashe knew that it didn't necessarily take professional sports titles or millions of dollars to make a difference. Ashe offered this often-quoted message to us all, trying to do the best we can to care for a world that needs to see the hope of Christ:

> "Start where you are. Use what you have. Do what you can."[8]

What would it look like for us to unite together, with what we have, to do what we can? Are we waiting for abundant resources or a perfect mission, or are we ready to make a difference in our communities right now? We all need to grab our bandages, oil, and wine, lock arms together, and serve together according to the mission and example of Jesus.

• Reflection Questions •

1. Think about a time when you were a part of a team that accomplished something big. How did that win or accomplishment make you feel toward other members of the team?

2. If you have been a part of a company, organization, or team that only focused on profits or winning, how did that make you feel?

3. What do you think about the example of the early church holding all things in common? Why do you believe the members of the early church sold items in order to help those in need? What would a similar model look like in your local community?

4. Thinking about your own company or organization, answer the question, "What do you all do here?"

5. What organizations or companies do you think do a good job of collective sight? What makes them great?

6. What ideas do you have for developing and exercising collective sight on your team?

7

OBSTRUCTIONS

*The Christian ideal has not been tried and found
wanting. It has been found difficult; and left untried.*[1]
—**G. K. Chesterton**

I remember when I got my dream car, a white 1999 Volkswagen GTI. As a fifteen-year-old, I would watch older guys in my neighborhood cruising around in their loud mufflered, boxy VW's and dream of owning one myself. Shortly after my sixteenth birthday, that dream was realized. This car had "435 air conditioning" (a.k.a., 4 windows down at 35 miles an hour), and a Sony Discman that played the latest Third Eye Blind or Puff Daddy tunes. I thought I was really something behind the wheel of that car. But on one fateful day, I drove down a popular road and ended my relationship with my VW.

A tree branch had snapped and fallen just perfectly in front of a traffic light, obstructing my vision from the impending red light. I barely had time to see the other car plow right into the side of me. I remember checking to see if the other driver was okay (they were), looking at the smashed side of my totaled vehicle, and then feeling a rush of anxiety over what my parents would say. Thankfully, they were understanding, but that was my last dance with my first vehicle.

We all need to be seen, and we all need to see others, but sometimes obstructions (like that snapped tree limb) inhibit our vision. As much as we want to be seen and have a desire to see others, seeing people can be difficult. Maybe you've tried to see others and you found yourself exhausted, rejected, or ignored. Maybe you've asked to be seen but received the same indifference that led you to isolation in the first place. In this chapter, we'll explore common obstructions that keep us from seeing others and learn how we can move beyond them as we make seeing people a part of our DNA.

Judas Ate Too

Jesus reclined at a table with His disciples for what is now known as the Last Supper. Imagery from Leonardo Da Vinci's *Last Supper* painting quickly comes to mind, but in first-century culture meal time involved gathering around a low table, leaning to a side with an elbow propped on the ground. Those eating sat closer to one another than we are accustomed to, and mealtime could last for hours. Such a gathering was intimate, meant to bring about conversation, listening, and laughter. When Jesus was accused of eating with sinners, it wasn't about food. It was about relationships, connection, and association.

Jesus's followers would have gathered for the Passover meal at this time each year, but Jesus had a new experience in mind. The Lord's Supper reinvented their familiar religious rhythm—one that reflected the new promise of forgiveness based on His own broken body and shed blood. Imagine for a moment Jesus reaching for the bread and holding it up to those around the table. When He broke the bread in His hand, did He envision the heavy cross nearly breaking His back as He marched up the hill? Did Jesus think of the nails in His hands and feet, or the crown of thorns piercing His scalp? The first Lord's Supper, for Jesus, was not merely a religious exercise. It was the foreshadowing of the final days of His life on earth.

Jesus's closest friends surrounded Him at the table. Between pieces of torn bread, He could look and see Peter, James, and John, His closest disciples. But He could also see Judas. The chief priests had been after Jesus to arrest Him, and Judas would be the one to give Him up. Days earlier, Judas went to the chief priests and asked them, "What would you give me if I deliver him over to you?" (Matt. 26:15). We don't know for sure, but it does seem that Judas took the first offer—an amount of silver worth about $500 today. Jesus walked with Judas. Fed him. Slept near him. Taught him. Loved him. And now, Judas sells Him to the first bidder for the price of an Xbox gaming console.

Still, Jesus gathered with Judas. Jesus told His disciples that one of them would betray Him, and Judas self-identified as the perpetrator. Jesus could have crushed Judas at any moment. Jesus could call down thousands upon thousands of angels to unleash God's wrath, but He didn't. He allowed Judas to eat at His table. I'm certainly not saying that Jesus overlooks sin, nor am I saying that Judas was forgiven. What I am saying, and what we see at the Last Supper, is that Jesus didn't immediately banish or punish those who sinned against Him. If you ever wondered what is meant in the Bible by the term *long-suffering*, Jesus's treatment of Judas is a helpful example. Jesus understood that not all would believe. He still saw Judas, fully knowing that Judas would reject Him. The Holy Spirit spoke these words through Paul that reflect the heart of Christ in 1 Corinthians 13:7: "Love bears all things, believes all things, hopes all things, endures all things."

If we want to go beyond surface level conversations, showing care and love like Jesus did, we have to identify the obstructions that prevent us from truly seeing others. We have to be willing to dig deeper until we discern the reasons behind our struggle to see. The truth is, it isn't always selfishness, or a lack of concern for others, that causes us to miss them instead of meeting them where they are. The journey of seeing others isn't easy. It can be exhausting, heartbreaking, and disappointing. It's no wonder so many feel unseen. We have to be willing to listen closely and honestly, and consider what obstructions are holding us back. Maybe now you'd be bold and humble enough to pray this simple prayer:

> *Jesus, I want to see people like You see people.*
> *I'm willing for You to do what's necessary in my*
> *heart to allow me to better see others around*
> *me. Show me where my vision is obstructed.*
> *Jesus, thank You for seeing me and sending me*
> *to see others.*

Stephen Overcame Obstructions

As we saw in chapter 6, the group charged with tending to the physical needs of widows were known as deacons, with Stephen serving as the first. The word *deacon* means "servant." Literally, the word was used to describe a person running who would kick up dust while performing errands. Deacons are dust kicker-uppers. They do what is necessary to provide care for others.

Stephen was a dust kicker-upper. When the church was asked to choose a person to head up the operation of caring for others, Stephen was the most prominent figure in their minds. He was described as a "man full of faith and the Holy Spirit" (Acts 6:5). Unfortunately, jealous religious figures rose up and told lies about Stephen and his ministry. He was falsely accused in front of the local government, and his reputation was destroyed. Even still, Stephen remained steadfast. The Scriptures say that despite persecution, his face shone like that of an angel (Acts 6:15).

Stephen had one last message to deliver. The man who was a walking, talking example of what it means to care could also teach sound doctrine. He preached a masterful sermon, weaving the salvation story of God throughout all of known Scripture. He even called out the religious elites who talked a great game of faith but didn't exhibit a life flowing from a heart transformed by the Lord.

He called them "stiff-necked people, uncircumcised in heart and ears" (Acts 7:51). Stephen shows us that we can be both radically caring toward others *and* unwavering in our convictions. "Stiff-necked" was a reference to the way a farmer felt about an ox who refused to be led. It's also a term the Lord used to describe unrepentant people in Exodus 33, Deuteronomy 9, and Nehemiah 9. God's people were (and still are) often resistant to His leadership. To be "uncircumcised in heart and ears" meant that while they physically exhibited the sign of the covenant (circumcision), they might as well not have been circumcised, because they didn't actually listen and respond to the Lord in their hearts. Stephen's bold words enraged his hearers, and they could hold back their anger no longer.

Just before the angry mob rushed toward him, Stephen saw a vision from above. He gazed into the sky and saw the glory of God, and Jesus standing at the right hand of God the Father (Acts 7:55). F. F. Bruce describes the vision this way: "Much more real to him in that moment than the angry gestures and cries of those around him was the presence of Jesus at God's right hand."[2] The standing position of Jesus is no accident. In almost every heavenly picture in the Bible we see Jesus sitting on the throne. But in this instance, He is standing in a posture of greeting His servant Stephen.

Don't you love Stephen? Ferociously caring, brilliant in doctrine, and boldly demonstrative of faith in Christ. Stephen busted through obstacles and moved the gospel forward. He stood up for the mission and work of Jesus, but he did so in love. His opposers eventually had enough of his preaching and took him outside the city and pelted him with stones. Stephen's final words were words of love and mercy. Acts 7:60 recounts, "And falling to his knees he cried out with a loud voice, 'Lord, do not hold this sin against them.' And when he had said this, he fell asleep."

Specific Obstructions

Each of the following obstructions will be presented as an assumption, a simple experience that is common to most of us. We'll also look at ways to navigate the obstruction and go beyond our comfort zone into the realm of faith, trusting that the Lord will use us in the lives of others.

Normal, Everyday Life

We're all busy, right? You're at the grocery store, list in hand, and it's time to conquer. Your schedule is packed with Zoom meetings, one-on-ones, and important projects. Or maybe homework, practice, and that part-time job dominate your day. We know how busy we are, and we project the pressure we feel onto others. We breeze past people throughout the day because we are on a mission. *Carpe diem*. Who has time to chat? We're all battling to find margin in our schedules. The philosopher Theophrastus said, "Time is the most valuable thing a man can spend."

Think about what happens in a conversation. Someone else can walk into our office, room, or within three feet of us and just start talking. Maybe you're brazen enough to completely ignore people. Most aren't. That means anyone can engage another person in a conversation. They can command time and mental effort with something as simple as "How are you doing today?" This is why high school students have learned the art of the simple answers: "Good." "Nothing." "Okay." It's enough to qualify as an answer but not enough to keep the conversation going. We often don't want to be slowed down, so we resist engaging with others.

In my student ministry days, we took a big group to Cedar Point Amusement Park, the roller coaster capital of the world. Unbeknownst to us, we joined the presence of the king himself that day—LeBron James. As we finished our ice cream between coaster rides, we looked in the distance and saw a huge crowd of people yelling, jumping, and taking pictures of a central figure. We couldn't quite tell who it was, because he was hidden in the center of a circle of really big, scary-looking guys. The job of the big, scary-looking guys was to keep the mob of middle schoolers away from LeBron. As the crowd shouted and asked for pictures, they walked alongside LeBron and shooed people away with both their words and their arms.

You probably don't have a circle of big, scary-looking guys to shoo people away from you. Anyone, at almost any time, can walk up and enter a conversation with you. You likely don't enjoy the pop-in, unannounced visit. Someone shows up at your house, your place of refuge, and expects conversation? How dare they!

There are simple ways to accomplish our daily tasks while also taking time to see people. Seeing people doesn't have to be about adding more appointments to our schedule. We can see people as we go. Here is one idea: when you write out your grocery list, write at the bottom of the list a simple statement: "See someone." Take your everyday task and add to it a simple goal: to show kindness and intentionality toward one person. Pick up the gallon of milk. As you do, slow down and focus on the grocery store clerk who helps you with the frustrating process of u-scan. Grade all the papers, but take time on one to provide a few sentences of a sincere, strength-based compliment. Go to the gym and show that elliptical machine who is the boss, but find one person along the way to engage with and respond with kindness to their story, if they share it. Seeing people isn't always about adding a new thing to your schedule. Instead, just ask yourself the question, "What am I already doing, and how can I see people along the way?"

I don't know how to help.

When our neighbor is in a difficult situation, and we consider the solution to be easy, we demonstrate a lack of empathy. Don't call what is difficult, easy. Seeing the world with empathetic eyes will emotionally motivate us to demonstrate real love and care. One of the conscious (or subconscious) obstructions to empathizing is a fear that we don't have the necessary wisdom, resources, or life experience to actually help someone. To that obstruction, here are two ways to move forward: start small and keep it simple.

First, seeing people doesn't require sage-like wisdom or piles of cash. Start small. Genuine care has become so uncommon that even the slightest move of care—like just listening—can make an impact. We won't ever be ready to care perfectly, so we can quit waiting and start anywhere. Little steps of love go a long way. If people wouldn't describe you as a person who usually looks to the needs of others, you're in a great place to start. Start small.

Second, keep it simple. We have a dear saint in our church who sees people by providing superior level biblical counseling at no cost. She has trained and studied for thousands of hours to glorify the Lord by seeing the Word of God further rule in the hearts of His followers. She says often that everyone who is a devoted follower of Jesus can counsel, and the process is simple: listen, offer hope, and pray. So simple, yet so profound. Listen, offer hope, and pray.

I'm already exhausted from helping.

Leading can be exhausting, whether you're in charge of an entire department or just trying to lead yourself through the week ahead. Leadership is taking what isn't—or what is chaotic—and bringing it to order and purpose. Being a student, parent, teacher, business leader, lawyer, salesperson, researcher, accountant, or analyst all involve bringing order to chaos, and that's hard. We're often left at the end of the day with spent minds, muscles, and emotions. Who has the energy to pour into the lives of others?

Charles R. Figley, the founder of the Traumatology Institute at Tulane University, has lectured on a concept known as "compassion fatigue." Compassion fatigue occurs when those who show care take on the suffering of those with whom they care. Figley goes as far to define it as an occupational hazard in certain fields, similar to the way an electrician would fear electric shock.[3] Kerry A. Schwanz, of Coastal Carolina University, warns that compassion fatigue doesn't just make it difficult to feel empathy for others. It also makes it difficult to cope with our own sources of stress and pain.[4] Researchers have concluded that those who work with people in a particular struggle often end up feeling the same kind of stress. Teachers feel the stress of their students. Mothers and fathers feel the stress of their children.

Thankfully, psychologists have recognized several helpful ways to deal with compassion fatigue, including recognition of the signs, self-care, and pressing into others in your community. Two additional components are most helpful in avoiding compassion fatigue, especially for those with a Christian worldview.

First, understand that we need to be seen, just as others need to be seen as well. When God created man, He said that it wasn't good that he was alone. We need others, and others need us. We cannot, and shouldn't, pour ourselves out on the altar of care with little or no genuine care from others in return. We need to see asking for care as a sign of strength and stability rather than a sign of weakness. When was the last time you asked someone, "Would you care for me in this way?" and then share a burden you are bearing? Do you invite others into your works of care? Do you humbly admit when your emotionally demanding occupation is wearing you thin? Share your story. Share your struggle. Please, don't just grind.

Second, we should embrace the concept of "compassion satisfaction." When we read and watch stories of great demonstrations of love and care, we're moved to go out and change the world. But then, we get anxious at the sheer number of needs out there. What if instead of trying to see everyone, we dedicated ourselves to see someone? What if instead of seeing everyone, we open ourselves up to the Lord using us to see anyone? Seeing *someone* or *anyone* is much more doable than seeing *everyone*. We should dream big, love large, and open ourselves up for God to do a great work in and through us, like in a context of collective sight from chapter 6. But what if we focused our effort in such a way that we could stand back after a period of time with a sense of "compassion satisfaction," knowing that we made ourselves available to the work of Jesus? Embracing our limitations may be the most freeing thing we can do.

Third, to fight compassion fatigue, prioritize time with Jesus. Foster and guard a regular rhythm in your life of praying, reading the Bible, and memorizing Scripture. We can't give others what we don't have ourselves, and we desire a vibrant relationship with Jesus that overflows to the world around us. Gather regularly with a local church, with all its strengths and quirks, and worship Jesus alongside others. If your local church is not a rallying point that reinvigorates your heart to see others, then something is amiss. Hebrews 10:24–25 shows us: "And let us consider how to stir up one another to love and good works, not neglecting to meet together, as is the habit of some, but encouraging one another, and all the more as you see the Day drawing near." We meet together to encourage, be encouraged, and stir one another up toward love and good works.

John the Baptist was Jesus's childhood friend. In fact, there is an encounter between Jesus and John the Baptist while they were still in their mothers' wombs where John leapt for joy at the sound of Jesus's mother Mary (Luke 1). They grew up together, made memories, and loved each other. Jesus experienced emotion, and He experienced emotion perfectly. Fast-forward to Matthew 13. Jesus is deep into His ministry on earth. He is healing, caring, and teaching.

Meanwhile, John the Baptist confronted Herod because Herod had an affair with his brother's wife. Herod didn't appreciate the rebuke, so he had John the Baptist imprisoned. At Herod's birthday party (thrown by himself), his daughter danced for everyone. The people loved it, and Herod rewarded her by saying she could have whatever she might ask. Herod's wife influenced the daughter to ask for the head of John the Baptist on a platter, and she got it.

The disciples buried the body of John, and then went to tell Jesus. The story picks up in Matthew 14:13:

> Now when Jesus heard this, he withdrew from
> there in a boat to a desolate place by himself.
> But when the crowds heard it, they followed
> him on foot from the towns.

Jesus is sad. And hurt. He grieves. He retreats and spends a short amount of time with His Father. But the people are still asking for His time, and teaching, and input. We never provide care in perfectly quarantined sections. One area of care bleeds over into all of life and we experience compassion fatigue. Jesus felt the need to take time to grieve. Recognize grief and caring for the grieving as the ministry burdens they are. Don't be afraid to admit it, and also don't be surprised when peoples' need for care keeps coming.

Some grow weary in their care, and some quit. Others turn to self-destructive behaviors to cope with their pain. But how did Jesus respond? "When he went ashore he saw a great crowd, and he had compassion on them and healed their sick" (Matt. 14:14). He didn't grow bitter. He didn't launch a campaign directed at Herod. He returned to the people He loved, felt compassion, and got back to work.

It's hard to see people who are difficult.

Is it your mother-in-law? A former coworker? A sister? Brother? We all know someone who is difficult to see. The thought of exercising care and kindness toward certain people is about as favorable as using a hedgehog as a loofah. It's difficult enough to tolerate certain people, much less go out of your way to care for them. They may have said things you will never forget. They may have done things with little (or a lot of) knowledge of how those things would hurt you. But let's cut to the heart of a Christlike response: we don't have to treat people the way they treat us.

Jesus didn't treat people the way He was treated. In Luke 23, an angry mob brought Jesus before Pilate, the governor of Judea. The mob shouted that Jesus misled the nation (although Jesus never lied to them), forbade the people from giving tribute to Caesar (Jesus didn't do this either), and claimed to be Messiah, a king (they were actually correct on this point). In light of these accusations, Jesus stood there, quietly and calmly before His accusers. This is the direct fulfillment of Isaiah 53:7: "He was oppressed, and he was afflicted, yet he opened not his mouth; like a lamb that is led to the slaughter, and like a sheep that before its shearers is silent, so he opened not his mouth."

Jesus did get angry. God is just, and He desires justice in the world. Psalm 82:3 says, "Give justice to the weak and the fatherless; maintain the right of the afflicted and the destitute." Amos 5:24 reads, "But let justice roll down like waters, and righteousness like an ever-flowing stream." There is a time for justice. But there is also a time for grace. Proverbs 15:1 reveals, "A soft answer turns away wrath, but a harsh word stirs up anger." Justice doesn't mean that we meet wrath with wrath. James 2:13 helps us here: "For judgment is without mercy to one who has shown no mercy. Mercy triumphs over judgment." We're also instructed in Romans 12:18, "If possible, so far as it depends on you, live peaceably with all."

Easier said than done, right? The ability to rise above provocation, offense, and insult comes only through prayer, the power of the Holy Spirit, and fresh dependence on the presence of Jesus. Colossians 1:21 teaches that we were once alienated and hostile in our minds toward God. We were once enemies of God, but God's own crucified and resurrected Son went to the Father on our behalf anyway. Jesus is our intercessor, or our go-between, to make us right with God. Jesus prays for us. What a humbling thought.

It's difficult to remain angry at people we serve. And it's difficult for others to remain angry at us while we serve them. We discussed earlier in the book that value is one of the three components of what it means to see someone (along with focus and response). Sometimes we value a person as a feeling. They're dear to us. We have affection for them. But sometimes, value is a thought. You can understand that someone is valuable in your mind, and that thought may later lead to a feeling. Voddie Baucham said, "Biblical love is an act of the will, accompanied by emotion, that leads to action on behalf of its object."[5] Value can begin as an act of the will, and emotion can later accompany our thoughts.

Imagine a person provokes you to anger, and you want to treat them the way you feel they are treating you. You want to defend, deflect, or destroy. But we remember the words of James, the brother of Jesus, who said, "Know this, my beloved brothers: let every person be quick to hear, slow to speak, slow to anger; for the anger of man does not produce the righteousness of God" (James 1:19–20). Here is a simple statement that can be helpful in times of provoked anger:

> You are important to me. And this is impor-
> tant to you. I want to slow down and listen
> carefully. I want to get this right.

Those four little sentences are easy for me to type here, alone in my office. They are very difficult for me to muster when I feel I'm wronged. I want to defend. I want to bring up evidence of my righteousness. I may even *be* right. But if I respond with an overwhelming desire to be heard, particularly if I want to be heard about being right, the conflict will never be resolved.

We can remember this: See them, even when you disagree. In addressing the angry customer, the frustrated student, or the disobedient child, see them, even when you disagree. Your temperature doesn't have to rise just because theirs is high. You don't put out a fire with more fire. Your disagreements may be fierce (and justified). However, your ability to move forward depends on one of you bringing grace to the conversation. See them, even when you disagree.

Am I saying you should let a person walk all over you? Absolutely not. There is a time to correct and rebuke (Prov. 8:5–6; 2 Tim. 4:2). Forgiveness is an important and complicated topic. We bear the wounds of the words and actions of others. What is beautiful is that you don't have to forgive someone to see them. But seeing someone may pave the path toward forgiveness.

If you spend enough time with any person, they'll give you plenty of reasons to be frustrated with them. If you spend enough time with a person, you'll give *them* plenty of reasons to be frustrated with *you*. Those who are unable to overlook frustration and resolve conflict will develop bitterness. Bitterness can be thought of as drinking poison and hoping that the other person dies. It can eat us alive from within. My wife, April, and I will often tell each other, "I'm sorry. I know I'm being a lot." The expression "being a lot" is a gentle way to communicate a spectrum of personal frustration. Tired from work. Entitled. Overlooked. Offended. Acknowledging awareness of my "a-lot-ness" sends a signal to my wife that I know how I'm acting (or reacting) and am prayerfully pushing through my silent adult temper tantrum.

Romans 2:4 tells us that it is God's kindness (not wrath or justice) that leads us to repentance. As image-bearers of our heavenly Father, it may be our kindness that will lead to the repentance of those we deem most difficult. We don't love people because they are lovable. We love people because they bear the image of our Creator—in all of their beauty and brokenness.

Dr. John Perkins had plenty of opportunities to deal with difficult people. His mother died when he was a baby, and his father abandoned him as a child. His brother died in an altercation with a police officer. He experienced all of the threats and pains common for a black man and leader in the civil rights era. Despite beatings, imprisonments, and death threats, he confronted injustice, racism, violence, and oppression. Despite receiving only a third grade education, Dr. Perkins has received more than a dozen honorary doctorates from more than a dozen universities. The circumstances surrounding his life have given him every opportunity to overlook others. Still, he spoke these words:

> You have to be a bit of a dreamer to imagine a world where love trumps hate—but I don't think being a dreamer is all that bad.... I'm an old man, and this is one of my dreams: that my descendants will one day live in a land where people are quick to confess their wrongdoing and forgive the wrongdoing of others and are eager to build something beautiful together.[6]

• Reflection Questions •

1. What barriers do you put up that discourage others from seeing you?

2. Have you experienced compassion fatigue? What helps refill your capacity for compassion?

3. What can the example of Jesus and the death of John the Baptist teach us about compassion fatigue?

4. Can you think of a person in your life (present or past) who you find difficult to see?

5. What obstructions in your life right now keep you from seeing people?

6. How might you move obstructions out of your life so that you can see others?

8

NOW, GO

"I wish it need not have happened in my time,"
said Frodo. "So do I," said Gandalf, "and so do
all who lived to see such times. But this is not
for them to decide. All we have to decide is
what to do with the time that is given us."[1]
—J. R. R. Tolkien, *The Fellowship of the Ring*

Our oldest son was born in a small village in Ethiopia. The Lord brought him to our family through adoption at the age of two. He has a name that was given to him by his birth parents, and it is beautiful, but it isn't a common name in the United States. We named him "Malin" (pronounced may-lin) because we liked the name. Not long after bringing him home, our family had a discussion at the dinner table about the meaning of our names. Our oldest daughter's name is Makenzie, which means "fair one." In fact, Makenzie is fair, and she is a treasure to know. My wife, April, discovered that her name is derived from the Latin word "to open," hence the month of April is a time for flowers to open and blossom. And true to her name, April has a life-giving spirit about her. Her smile and presence open up a room.

I'd never looked up the meaning of my own name, Dustin. Every Dustin I've met has had one thing in common—we gave our mom a hard time, so I thought that might be the meaning of my name. Kidding aside, I learned that the name Dustin originates from an English surname, which is derived from the Old Norse name *Tursten*. Tursten is a combination of the words *Thor* (a powerful being of lightning, thunder, and strength) and *steinn*, which means stone. Combining Thor and stone together gives the name Dustin the meaning of "brave warrior."

I wish I could tell you we prayed and fasted for days for the Lord to give us the perfect name for each of our children. We didn't. Providentially, it all worked out. Such was the case with our son Malin. I distinctly remember watching April look up his name, and immediately upon reading the words on the screen, tears came to her eyes. She looked toward me, and told me that my eldest son's name means "brave little warrior."

Names are powerful. Our heavenly Father bears several different names in the Bible. He is so uniquely awesome that it takes many names to begin to communicate the depth and breadth of who He is. Sometimes God reveals a specific name to His people. The Lord told Moses to call Him Yahweh, which means "I am who I am." "Yahweh" refers to the eternal nature of God. He always has been and always will be. Other names of God come from people's interactions with Him. In Hebrew culture, a name is not so much a simple identifier as it is something that points to the whole of someone's identity.

Hagar, a young Egyptian servant girl, gave a name to the Lord. We see that story unfold in Genesis 12–17. Hagar served a wealthy couple, Abraham and Sarah. God made a promise to Abraham that He would make him the father of a great nation, even many nations. The Lord appears to Abraham in Genesis 15 and tells him: "Fear not . . . I am your shield; your reward shall be very great" (v. 1). Abraham wasn't always grateful, and he reminds the Lord that He had never come through on His promise to give him children. Graciously, the Lord directs Abraham to go outside and look up at the countless number of stars in the sky. God tells him, "So shall your offspring be" (Gen. 15:5).

Abraham and Sarah grew impatient waiting on the Lord and took matters into their own hands. Abraham was eighty-six years old, and Sarah was ninety-six years old. They'd been waiting on the Lord for quite some time, and they weren't getting any younger. Sarah commanded her servant, Hagar, to marry Abraham and give them a child. Hagar conceived, causing Sarah to lash out at Abraham and to despise Hagar. The text in Genesis 16 tells us that Sarah dealt harshly with Hagar, and Hagar ran away from them.

An angel of the Lord came to Hagar in the wilderness, bringing a word of comfort and promise. The angel instructed Hagar to return to her home and assured her that she would have the opportunity to be a mother to many children. It was this interaction with an angel from the Lord that moved Hagar to call the Lord, *El Roi*, or "The God who sees." Hagar said, "I have now seen the One who sees me" (Gen. 16:13 NIV).

Embracing the truth that God sees us is the most powerful motivation we have for seeing others. Our God sees us. Right now. He sees every moment of our past and every moment of our future. Matthew 10:30 shows us that our heavenly Father knows the number of hairs on our head—whether that number is many or very few. Despite our sins, shortcomings, mistakes, and rebellion, our God chooses to see us. He is El Roi, the God who sees, and He sees us at our best and our worst. And He loves us.

If we are to see people—not just in a single moment of sympathetic response, but through a lifestyle of abounding kindness, love, and intentionality—we must fan into the flame our awareness of God's love toward us. You may have been raised in a religious tradition with a tone that puts God at arm's length or depicts people as constantly in the penalty box with their heavenly Father. It is true we are sinners, but God made a way for us to come confidently into His presence: Jesus. Romans 5:8 tells us, "But God shows his love for us in that while we were still sinners, Christ died for us." Perhaps it bears dwelling on the part that reads "*while* we were still sinners."

Perseverance in seeing others comes from better understanding our identity of who we are in Christ. Jesus tells us clearly in John 5:24, "Truly, truly, I say to you, whoever hears my word and believes him who sent me has eternal life. He does not come into judgment, but has passed from death to life." We are no longer dead to God and living in sin. We are alive to God and dead to sin. We've been made new. "Therefore, if anyone is in Christ, he is a new creation. The old has passed away; behold, the new has come" (2 Cor. 5:17). We are a new creation, with good deeds determined by God for us to go and do.

We aren't valuable because we achieve. Our worth is inherent in who we are as image-bearers of God. Don't buy into the idea that you must achieve your value. This isn't the way our heavenly Father views us. Achieving to gain value will lead to feverish, angst-ridden toil. Achieving from an understanding of value will cultivate a sense of peace and perseverance.

Think about the people you influence, right now—friends, children in your classroom, employees, roommates, a fiancé, or spouse. Here is why we must get value and achievement in the correct order. If we first treat others as valuable, their achieving will flow from a sense of care and connection. If people get the sense from us that they must achieve in order for us to show them they are valuable, we create an unclear, toil-ridden environment of approval. Instead, let's see others by showing them we understand their inherent value as image-bearers, then watch the beautiful process of God's work in and through them.

In the remainder of this chapter I want to offer more practical ideas for how you might see people in your daily life. They build on the practical ideas offered in previous chapters. Not all of the ideas will be for you immediately, but I hope you'll take some inspiration from them. Pick one and try it. Or pick one and adapt it to better suit your situation and personality. After you've tried one, I hope you'll consider using the practical portions of this book as a resource to come back to in order to refresh how you and those around you can attempt to see people the way God sees all of us.

To get started, here's one easy way to show others that they are valuable. Tell the people you care about—wait for it . . .—that you care about them. It isn't a groundbreaking new idea. But how often do we stop, slow down, and affirm intentionally and directly our care for others? Call a friend (don't text) out of the blue and say, "_____ (say their name), this might seem random, but I was thinking of how much your friendship means to me. I'm so glad that for the person that you are. You're in this world, and I'm grateful."

Plan to See People

We all have important meetings on our calendar. We make plans to check off our endless to-do lists. Similarly, we need to make a plan to see people. The people around us are too valuable for us only to see them when it's convenient for us. Here are several ways that we can intentionally plan to see others.

"Who do I plan to see this week?" In whatever your weekly planning time looks like, ask yourself that simple question. Then, write the name down. Maybe even say out loud, "This week I plan to see _____." There are lots of names that you could write down. But focus on one instead of attempting to dilute your attention across many people. Intentionality, by definition, implies a directed effort. For at least one week, aim your effort toward a specific person. Pray for them. Consider their value as an image-bearer of God. Slow down and focus on them. Remember your conversation with them and think about how to respond.

Next, create a list of names of the people who are closest to you. If you are a digital creature like me, a note on your phone might be the most accessible, but if you're a paper journal type, by all means use that. The key is ease of use. Beside their name, type out one characteristic you admire about them. Be specific, sincere, and strengths based. Use this list to leverage the little pieces of time in your day. Take advantage of downtime in airports, while driving, or waiting for appointments and knock out 3–5 messages or calls. Don't fill in the cracks of your time with scrolling. Fill your time with seeing.

From Stranger to Seeing

Contact tracing became an important part of fighting the COVID-19 pandemic. If a person tests positive, or if they are in close contact with someone who tests positive, we are asked to make a list of those with whom we had recent contact so they may take proper precautions. These lists of interactions could get extensive depending on the number of people we see each day. What if we made a list, not for contact tracing purposes, but for the purpose of considering who we can see?

Sit down with your calendar and think back over your day or week. Think about every single person with whom you made contact—the barista, doctor, barber, teacher, supervisor, bus driver, dog walkers, Zoom call colleagues, fellow parents at sporting events, etc. Go hour by hour and place by place, and write down every person you remember coming across. If you don't know their name, write down a short description (and then make it a task to learn their name). At the top of the list, put the letters V-F-R for value, focus, and respond. Next to each name, write down one way that you can respond to each person. This is an opportunity to step back and think creatively about how you can go over-the-top in kindness and thoughtfulness.

A sister in Christ once said told the story of sitting on a plane in front of a young mom who was trying to quiet a screaming baby with everyone eyeing her. Seeing that the mom was exhausted, the older woman whispered, "Could you use a little help?" Tears welled in the mother's eyes as she nodded. The dear lady took the little one to the rear of the plane and swung him back-and-forth in her arms and sang over him as grandma-types do, and when she knew the little one was in a deep sleep, she took him back and that precious young woman was out cold, sleeping in her seat. She got to hold that little sweetie for an hour and created a lasting memory.

I once heard my friend Dan Dewitt say, "A need seen is an assignment given." He mentioned it in passing as a small part of a sermon, but I've never forgotten it. To be honest, the saying gets under my skin when I'm busy or focused on my own tasks. I can't necessarily stop at every need I see, but I can take up at least some of the assignments that my world presents. Moms and dads—the next time you gather at your dinner table, present to your crew this simple truth: "A need seen is an assignment given." Ask them if they agree and discuss how you can make meetings needs a part of the rhythm of your family.

Team Up

Team up with others to see people. Roommates, friends, fellow church members, parents, children, and neighbors can become co-conspirators in kindness toward others. Start with "Who did you see today?" This is an open-ended, nonjudgmental nudge for sharing encouraging stories. If we know we will be asked this question, we'll be more likely to keep our heads up and eyes on others around us. This question goes well with the classic highs and lows, peaks and valleys, roses and thorns type question. You could also abbreviate the question as "WDYST" and post the abbreviation as artwork, on bulletin boards, and in email signatures.

The "who did you see today?" question can become a part of teachers' meetings, date nights, and even company check-ins. Asking this question reminds us that people are just as important as profit. Employees should be reminded that every person who walks through the doors of the store, every client they see on a Zoom call, every fellow employee is a real person with struggles similar to our own. Notice the human element in every business interaction. Organizational leaders also should regularly share about people they see. We all need to see people. We all need to be seen.

Another question we can ask is, "How do you need to be seen this week?" We have appointments, expectations, tests, and looming news that weigh heavy on our hearts. The heaviness of life can cause us to be quick-tempered or withdrawn. Communicating our burdens when answering that question will set others up to share specific grace and encouragement. On Sunday night, take time to ask your roommates, "How do you need to be seen this week?" The question implies a posture of seeing others. When we exchange those kinds of prompts with one another, we're communicating that we want to see people, and we're willing to specifically see people the way they want to be seen. Again, don't wait to be the kindest person in the universe. Start somewhere, start simple, and stay at it.

We can also coach one another in an effort to better see others. Coaching involves giving instruction and asking key questions. Seeing people includes showing value, drawing in with focus, and responding to real needs. When you gather a team for a mid-season meeting, or meet before a shift, or sit around a conference room table to discuss strategy or to debrief, make seeing people a key part of your oversight. Here are three coaching questions that can be helpful:

- How did you show others that they are valuable?
- What did you do to block out distractions and focus on those you are leading or serving alongside?
- How did you respond to the needs of others this week?

Each of those three questions implies unselfishness. It's close to impossible to see others while simultaneously focusing on yourself. Seeing others moves us from self-preservation, self-pity, and self-promotion and into the real lives of our neighbors.

Set Reminders

An old Chinese proverb says that "the faintest ink is more powerful than the strongest memory." When we see an opportunity to respond to the needs of others, we can have the greatest of intentions, but we need a plan to make a difference. We need reminders. People are important enough to put on our schedule. Some may find it disingenuous or mechanical to set a reminder to reach out on a certain interval, but the heart and motive behind scheduling reminders is that people are too important to leave to our own memory and distractions. Setting reminders to reach out to others on a weekly, biweekly, monthly, or quarterly basis will show them, over time, how much they're valued by you. It's one way to help us focus.

Set reminders on your phone to make an encouraging phone call, send a text message, or simply pray for a recent prayer request. We set reminders to water the plants, take out the trash, and check on food in the oven. I had a conversation this week with a dear friend whose father suddenly passed away. My friend was concerned for his mother, who would be in a home all by herself for the first time since their wedding fifty years ago. Instead of leaving care of his mother up to his memory, I encouraged my friend to set a reminder on his phone for every Tuesday and Thursday afternoon at 2 p.m. to make a call to her. I'd have to imagine that his mother would soon look forward to hearing from her son at these regular times.

The follow-up response we give to others doesn't have to be long. Sometimes I'll even send a message and say something to the effect of "No need to respond. I know you're a busy person. I just wanted you to know that I'm thinking of and praying for you today." If you're a part of a Bible study, community group, or have close Christian friends, take the prayer request time as a prompt to set reminders to reach out to others to let them know you're actually praying for them. Be specific. Say, "Today, I prayed for _____. Love you, brother/sister."

I shared with a friend in our church that I was working to get in better shape after a back surgery. We discussed workout routines and dreaded meal planning. We discussed how brisket and mac and cheese tastes much better than grilled chicken and broccoli. I didn't think much of the conversation until the next Monday morning when I received a text asking, "How are the workouts and meal prep?" The next Monday, I received a similar message, and I have every Monday since that conversation. I'm thankful for my friend seeing me.

See the People Closest to You

Those closest to us need to know that we see them. Proximity does not equal sight. I've counseled dozens of couples who often say the same thing, "We live in the same house, sleep right next to each other, but we've been growing apart for some time." There are many reasons why couples and other close relationships grow apart, but one thing they have in common is that at some point along the way, one or both persons start to feel unseen. When conflict arises, typically the issues will revolve around a lack of seeing one another. If a roommate leaves dirty dishes in the sink, the other person feels like their desire for cleanliness goes unseen. If one spouse spends too much money on frivolous items, the other person feels like they aren't committed to savings and the desires of the other person. Instead, what if we proactively initiated conversations that demonstrated a desire to see the other person?

- I had a difficult day today, and you showed me mercy in my stress. Thank you.
- I see you working hard for our family.
- I know that I haven't been easy to live with today. Thanks for your grace toward me.
- This is a difficult season for you. I want you to know that I see that.
- I understand that this issue is important to you. I want to hear from you.

These types of affirmations imply I want to understand life in your shoes. They're a demonstration of empathy. Embrace the mentality that the person is more important than your position or the problem at hand. See the person and, when you can, overlook the problem. Proverbs 19:11 shows us, "Good sense makes one slow to anger, and it is his glory to overlook an offense."

Conflict is often the result of a lack of feeling seen. Think about the relationship struggles you've faced in the past six months at work or at home.

- Did you feel valued?
- Did you feel like others dropped distractions and spent time focusing on you?
- Do you feel that others responded to your real needs?

If you answered no to one (or more) of those questions. it's likely you felt unseen. Thinking again about a recent conflict, turn the mirror around for a moment, and ask yourself these questions.

- Did I make the other person feel valued?
- Did I drop distractions in order to spend time focusing on them?
- Did I respond to their real needs?

You don't have to agree with a person in order to see them. Don't be distracted by a desire to be right, heard, or to win an argument. Begin to set these desires aside in an effort to see the other person. Be the initiator in seeking forgiveness. The root of the problem may only be 1 percent your responsibility (it's possibly more), but a willingness to see the person along with the problem paves the way to reconciliation.

Hope

We must be willing to be inconvenienced. We must be people who will slow down, draw in, and respond. People often feel pushed away and stepped over in our world today. While everyone else is scrambling to the top of a ladder, we have to be people who will go lower, drawing others in and lifting them up. It's exactly what our God did for us, and exactly what He is calling us to do for others.

Parents of adult children often ask me to pray for their wayward children. I hear stories of children who grew up going to church and hearing all about Jesus, but for one reason or another, they've chosen not to go the way of Jesus. Maybe you're reading this, and you have a child who would fit this description. It's heartbreaking, and their mother and father pray for them with tears. Here is why seeing people is eternally important. In workplaces, ballfields, and neighborhoods these wayward souls are probably near us—and it's up to you and me to see them. We are being prayed for by those precious moms and dads who would do anything to see their adult child come to faith. See them. Slow down. Put down the phone. Say hello. Invite them over. Bear the awkwardness of new relationships for the sake of the value of a human soul who is desperately loved by their earthly and heavenly Father.

Every day, people around us are wondering if they are redeemable. People feel stuck, anxious, confused, enraged, and lonely all at the same time. We are the ones, the gospel light-bearers sent to image-bearers to express the love of their heavenly Father. No life is unredeemable. No one has gone too far outside the reach of their heavenly Father. Psalm 86:15 declares, "But you, O Lord, are a God merciful and gracious, slow to anger and abounding in steadfast love and faithfulness."

German painter Moritz Retzsch painted the marvelous work commonly known as *Checkmate*. In broad strokes of oil, we see Satan playing chess with a man who appears frustrated and defeated by the father of lies. The chessboard sits atop of the base of a fountain and is surrounded by imagery contributing to the themes of salvation and eternity. Retzsch is known for such imagery, and he also has been known to hide puzzles throughout his works.

If people are honest, many feel like that seemingly defeated opponent. They've tried and toiled but come up short on salvation and significance. Some then devote themselves to pleasure because at least it provides for a moment. Others spiral into fits of anxiety and depression. A small portion reach for achievement and notoriety. But in the end, our human solutions just add one loss after another to the scoreboard.

A tournament of chess champions was once held in Paris where *Checkmate* hung on display in the Louvre. Curators from the museum had an idea to welcome chess champions to the museum in order to solicit expert perspectives on the painting. One champion after another filed by the nearly 200-year-old painting. One of the final champions stopped suddenly and focused in closer to the description mounted next to the work. He looked back and forth between the painting and description several times before the curator inquired as to his insight. The champion responded, "Well, either the title of the painting will have to change, or the painting will have to change." The curator asked, "How so?" To which the champion responded, "My dear, the king has one more move."

Because of the victory Christ delivered on the cross and the power of His resurrection, our King has one more move. He is not finished, we are not defeated, and He will return again—not as a lowly carpenter, but as a risen warrior King. We are heralds of this message, stewards of the good news of Christ. The King has one more move, and we're here not merely to exist, but to advance His message of hope to a world that desperately needs to see it. They'll see it when we see them. When they do, may we speak the words of the one who gives living water so they may thirst no more.

• Reflection Questions •

1. Do you know the meaning of your name? How is that name meaningful to you?

2. When you think about God as El Roi, the God who sees, how does that strike you?

3. Which one of the practical plans for seeing people will you use this week?

4. Think about a recent conflict. Did you feel like the other person valued or focused on you? Did you feel like the other

person responded to your needs? How might a lack of feeling seen prompt you to better see others in conflicts?

5. What other ideas do you have for planning to see others in your life?

6. Has there been a time in your life where you felt like you were at a dead end, but it turned out that the King had one more move?

7. Who do you know right now who needs to know that the King has one more move?

NOTES

Chapter 1

1. Priyanjali Narayan, "Six instances when Mr. Rogers made the world a better place by being his wholesome self," *Upworthy*, March 21, 2023, https://scoop.upworthy.com/six -times-mr-rogers-made-the-world-a-better-place#.

2. Rachel E. Greenspan, "Inside the Unlikely Friendship That Inspired a Beautiful Day in the Neighborhood," *TIME*, November 22, 2019, https://time.com/5733017/a-beautiful -day-in-the-neighborhood-true-story/.

3. Derek Thompson, "Why American Teens Are So Sad," *The Atlantic*, April 11, 2022, https://www.theatlantic.com /newsletters/archive/2022/04/american-teens-sadness- depression-anxiety/629524/.

4. "Sawubona!," Loom International, https://www.loom international.org/sawubona/.

5. For a more thorough explanation of this Zulu greeting, see this TED Talk by Roche Mamabolo: https://youtu.be/xpqU9 MtL8MI?si=8TffsAZZtxaWHvu6.

6. David L. Strayer and Frank A. Drews, "Cell-Phone–Induced Driver Distraction," *Association for Psychological Science*, vol. 16, no. 3 (2007), http://appliedcognition.psych.utah.edu/publica- tions/cellphone.pdf.

Chapter 2

1. C. S. Lewis, *The Lion, the Witch and the Wardrobe* (1950; repr., New York: HarperCollins, 2000), 79–80.

2. "Apostle Peter Cringes While Reading Gospel Accounts of All the Dumb Stuff He Did," *Babylon Bee*, May 10, 2019, https://babylonbee.com/news/apostle-peter-embarrassed-while-reading-about-all-the-dumb-stuff-he-did-in-the-gospels.

3. Dane C. Ortlund, *Gentle and Lowly: The Heart of Christ for Sinners and Sufferers* (Wheaton, IL: Crossway, 2020), 39.

4. Thomas Goodwin, *The Heart of Christ* (Edinburgh: Banner of Truth, 2011), 107.

5. Scott Sauls, *A Gentle Answer: Our "Secret Weapon" in an Age of Us against Them* (Nashville: Nelson Books, 2020), 5.

6. "Derwin Gray on the Pushback against Racial Diversity and How to Build a Truly Multi-Ethnic Organization," *Carey Nieuwhof Leadership Podcast*, no. 429, July 14, 2021, https://careynieuwhof.com/episode429/.

7. John Powell's final sermon can be seen at "EBC Summer in the Psalms – Psalm 72," YouTube, July 5, 2020, https://www.youtube.com/watch?v=r4EIz5mhHfQ.

Chapter 3

1. Tim Keller went home to be with the Lord in 2023. In his book *Every Good Endeavor: Connecting Your Work to God's Work* he said this to men and women living out the work of the gospel in the world. Tim Keller, *Every Good Endeavor: Connecting Your Work to God's Work* (New York: Penquin Books, 2014).

2. ". . . everyone who is called by my name, whom I created for my glory, whom I formed and made" (Isa. 43:7).

3. Wayne Grudem, *Systematic Theology: An Introduction to Biblical Doctrine* (Grand Rapids: Zondervan, 1994), 490.

4. "Plumb Line #1: The Gospel Is Not Just the Diving Board; It's the Pool," J.D. Greear Ministries, July 27, 2016, https://jdgreear.com/plumb-line-1-the-gospel-is-not-just-the-diving-board-its-the-pool/.

5. Augustine, *Confessions*, 1.1.1.

6. Ray Ortlund and Sam Allberry, "Hey Pastors! You're Not Crazy!," The Gospel Coalition, August 16, 2021, https://bit.ly/3A TYoxN.

7. Russell Moore's book *Losing Our Religion: An Altar Call for Evangelical America* speaks more extensively to this point.

8. Alistair Begg, "The Man on the Middle Cross Said I Can Come," YouTube, November 20, 2019, https://www.youtube.com/watch?v=xk9wgJBoEd8.

Chapter 4

1. Frederick Buechner, *Whistling in the Dark: A Doubter's Dictionary* (New York: HarperCollins, 1993), 17.

2. A. W. Tozer, *The Knowledge of the Holy* (New York: HarperCollins, 1978), 1.

3. "The Human Eye—for His Glory!" YouTube, August 28, 2021, https://www.youtube.com/watch?v=eYu91QbvVqE&t=11s.

4. Mary Schaller and John Crilly, *The 9 Arts of Spiritual Conversations: Walking Alongside People Who Believe Differently* (Carol Stream, IL: Tyndale House Publishers, 2016), 48.

5. Nicholas G. Carr, *The Shallows: What the Internet Is Doing to Our Brains* (New York: W. W. Norton & Company, 2011), 6–7.

6. Nicholas Carr, "Does the Internet Make You Dumber?," *Wall Street Journal*, June 5, 2010, https://www.wsj.com/articles /SB10001424052748704025304575284981644790098.

7. Madeline Kennedy, "How much screen time is too much?," *Insider*, October 16, 2020, https://www.insider.com/how-much -screen-time-is-too-much.

8. "The Loneliness Epidemic Persists: A Post-Pandemic Look at the State of Loneliness among U.S. Adults," https://news room.thecignagroup.com/loneliness-epidemic-persists-post -pandemic-look.

9. Elena Renken, "Most Americans Are Lonely, and Our Workplace Culture May Not Be Helping," NPR, January 23, 2020, https://www.npr.org/sections/health-shots/2020/01/23/798676465/most-americans-are-lonely-and-our-workplace-culture-may-not-be-helping.

10. Daniel A. Cox, "The Sate of American Friendship: Change, Challenges, and Loss," May 2021 American Perspectives Survey, https://www.americansurveycenter.org/research/the-state-of-american-friendship-change-challenges-and-loss/.

11. Caitlin Johnson, "Cutting Through Advertising Clutter," CBS News, September 17, 2006, https://www.cbsnews.com/news /cutting-through-advertising-clutter/.

12. Louise Story, "Anywhere the Eye Can See, It's Likely to See an Ad," *New York Times*, January 15, 2007, https:// web.archive.org/web/20200320191358/https:/www.nytimes .com/2007/01/15/business/media/15everywhere.html.

13. Bob Goff, *Love Does: Discover a Secretly Incredible Life in an Ordinary World* (Nashville: Thomas Nelson, 2012), 8.

14. "Me Monster," Brian Regan, YouTube, July 5, 2012, https://youtu.be/vymaDgJ7KLg?si=Yj9or7KLYUcwWC7y.

15. Doug Pollock, *God Space: Where Spiritual Conversations Happen Naturally* (Loveland, CO: Group Publishing, 2009), 38.

16. "The Starry Night": Biola University Commencement Address, May 2021," https://makotofujimura.com/writings/the-starry-night-biola-university-commencement-address-may-2012.

17. "The Starry Night."

18. Melissa McQuillan, *Van Gogh* (London: Thames & Hudson, 1989).

19. David Sweetman, *Van Gogh: His Life and His Art* (New York: Crown Publishing, 1990), 342–43; Jan Hulsker, *The Complete Van Gogh: Paintings, Drawings, Sketches* (New York: H. N. Abrams, 1980), 480–83.

Chapter 5

1. Ken Gire, *Moments with the Savior* (Grand Rapids: Zondervan, 1998), 218.

2. Joel B. Green, *The Gospel of Luke* (Wm. B. Eerdmans Publishing Co.), 639.

3. Eugene Peterson, *The Jesus Way: A Conversation on the Ways That Jesus Is the Way* (Grand Rapids: William B. Eerdmans, 2007), 67–68.

4. Don Carson in Justin Taylor, "Who Is the Ultimate Good Samaritan?," The Gospel Coalition, September 9, 2013, https://www.thegospelcoalition.org/blogs/justin-taylor/who-is-the-ultimate-good-samaritan/.

5. Definition of "lavish," *Oxford Languages*, https://www.google.com/search?q=lavish+definition&rlz=1C5CHFA_enUS9

28US928&oq=lavish+defi&aqs=chrome.0.0i20i263i433i512j0i51
2j69i57j0i512l2j69i60l3.2531j1j9&sourceid=chrome&ie=UTF-8.

6. *The Long Goodbye: The Kara Tippetts Story*, directed by Jay Lions, released March 12, 2019, https://www.youtube.com/watch?v=GFaKwZeDJH4.

7. Alison Abbott, "COVID's mental-health toll: how scientists are tracking surge in depression," *Nature*, February 3, 2021, https://www.nature.com/articles/d41586-021-00175-z.

8. Abbott, "COVID's mental-health toll."

9. Lea Winerman, "The Mind's Mirror," *Monitor on Psychology* 36, no. 9 (October 2005), https://www.apa.org/monitor/oct05/mirror.

10. Seth Godin blog, "Our upside-down confusion about fairness," January 15, 2014, https://seths.blog/2014/01/our-upside-down-confusion-about-fairness/.

11. TedxTalks, "Sawubona, we see you | Roche Mamabola," YouTube, September 23, 2019, https://www.youtube.com/watch?v=xpqU9MtL8MI.

12. Ramsey Solutions, "The State of Debt Among Americans," conducted in 2017, https://www.ramseysolutions.com/debt/state-of-debt-among-americans-research.

13. "This Church Opens Wide Her Doors," DashHouse.com, Ray Ortlund's adaptation of James Boice, https://www.dashhouse.com/201498this-church-opens-wide-her-doors/.

Chapter 6

1. Joel Goldberg, "It Takes a Village to Determine the Origins of an African Proverb," NPR, July 30, 2016, https://www.npr

.org/sections/goatsandsoda/2016/07/30/487925796/it-takes-a
-village-to-determine-the-origins-of-an-african-proverb.

2. Quotation originally published in Frederick Buechner's *Wishful Thinking: A Theological ABC*, https://www.frederick
buechner.com/quote-of-the-day/2017/7/18/vocation.

3. "Mental Health Policies and Programmes in the Workplace," World Health Organization, 2005, https://apps
.who.int/iris/bitstream/handle/10665/43337/9241546794_eng
.pdf?sequence=1&isAllowed=y.

4. Ken Curtis and Josh Barnett, "A Look at the Early Christian Church," *Christianity Today*, August 18, 2023, www
.christianity.com/jesus/early-church-history/early-churches/
how-was-the-early-church-perceived.html.

5. Daniel Goleman, "Millennials: The Purpose Generation," https://www.kornferry.com/insights/this-week-in-leadership
/millennials-purpose-generation.

6. Talk given at Champion Forest Connect event, November 15, 2021.

7. "Your Employees Care about Social Responsibility—You Should Too," Center for Creative Leadership, November 24, 2021, ccl.org/articles/leading-effectively-articles/your-workers-care
-about-social-responsibility-you-should-too/.

8. "'Start Where You Are. Use What You Have. Do What You Can.'—Arthur Ashe," University of Pacific, May 12, 2022, https://pacific.edu.ni/start-where-you-are-use-what-you-have
-do-what-you-can-arthur-ashe/#:~:text="Start%20Where%20
You%20Are.,Arthur%20Ashe%20%2D%20University%20of%20
Pacific.

Chapter 7

1. G. K. Chesterton, *What's Wrong with the World* (New York: Dodd, Mead, and Company, 1912), 48.

2. F. F. Bruce, *The Book of Acts: New International Commentary on the New Testament* (Grand Rapids: Eerdmans, 1988), 154.

3. Debbie L. Stoewen, "Moving from Compassion Fatigue to Compassion Resilience, Part 2: Understanding Compassion Fatigue," *Canadian Veterinary Journal* 60, no. 9 (September 2019): 1004–1006, https://www.ncbi.nlm.nih.gov/pmc/articles/PMC6697064/#:~:text=The%20world%20renowned%20traumatologist%2C%20Charles,caregiving%20environment"%20(7).

4. Kerry A. Schwanz, "Compassion Fatigue Resilience: Taking Care of Yourself While Caring about Others," National Health Register of Health Service Psychologists, 2022, https://ce.nationalregister.org/wp-content/uploads/2022/01/Compassion-Fatigue-Resilience-National-Register.pdf.

5. "Love Is an Act of the Will—Voddie Baucham Sermons," YouTube, June 10, 2023, https://youtu.be/QkM3_AJFcnI?si=oAh3sK1upZp0oVBH.

6. John M. Perkins, *Dream with Me: Race, Love, and the Struggle We Must Win* (Grand Rapids, MI: Baker Books, 2018), 169.

Chapter 8

1. J. R. R. Tolkien, *The Fellowship of the Ring* (New York: Ballantine Books, 1981), 82.